THE FRANZ BARDON TRADITION

Interviews with Experienced Practitioners

THE FRANZ BARDON COMMUNITY

(Foreword by Martin Faulks)

COMPILED BY FALCON BOOKS PUBLISHING

Published by Falcon Books Publishing Ltd
Cover design by Justin B
First Printing: 2021

FALCON BOOKS PUBLISHING LTD
*St Neots Masonic Hall 166 School Lane, Eaton Socon,
St Neots, England, PE19 8EH.*

www.falconbookspublishing.com

Ordering Information:
Hardback copies are available on the Falcon Books Publishing website:

www.falconbookspublishing.com

ISBN-10: 1-8384598-6-4
ISBN-13:978-1-8384598-6-4

Proofread by Kendal Moore

Dedication

This book is dedicated to the great Magician, Franz Bardon and all of who have made it their goal to pursue his teachings for the betterment of themselves and humanity.

FALCON BOOKS PUBLISHING TITLES

The Spirit of Magic- Rediscovering the Heart of this Sacred Art, by Virgil, Second Edition. 2016.

The Path of the Mystic – Special Edition for Franz Bardon Practitioners, by Ray del Sole. 2017.

Enlightened Living, Martin Faulks. 2017.

The Elemental Equilibrium, Virgil. 2017.

The Cover Side to Initiation, Virgil. 2018.

Stories of Magic and Enchantment, William R. Mistele. 2018.

Mermaid Tales, William R. Mistele. 2018.

Adepthood, Martin Faulks. 2018.

The Four Elements, William R. Mistele. 2019.

The Gift to Be Simple, Virgil. 2020.

The Moon Zone, Nenad Djordjevic -Talerman. 2020.

Corpus Hermetticum, The Power & Wisdom of God, Marsilio Ficino (Includes the Asclepius Dialogue) Translated by Maxwell Lewis Latham. 2020.

360 Heads of the Earth Zone; Volume I Spring, Nenad Djordjevic -Talerman. 2021.

Hermetic Meditation, Martin Faulks. 2021.

CONTENTS

Falcon Books Publishing Titles 3
Contents 5
Abbreviations 6
Foreword 7
Preface 11
CHAPTER 1: André Consciência 15
CHAPTER 2: Crystalf Maibach 53
ChAPTER 3: David Paul Coleman 69
CHAPTER 4: Julia Griffin 83
CHAPTER 5: Justin B The Magician 93
CHAPTER 6: Martin Faulks 113
CHAPTER 7: Nenad Djordjevic-Talerman 129
CHAPTER 8: Ray del Sole 149
CHAPTER 9: Virgil 163
CHAPTER 10: William R. Mistele 187

ABBREVIATIONS

EGZ- Earth Girdling Zone
HGA – Higher Guardian Angel
IIH – *Initiation Into Hermetics,* Franz Bardon
KTQ – *Key to The Qabbalah*, Franz Bardon
VOM – Vacancy of Mind
VF– Vital Force

FOREWORD

“No barriers to learning” is a motto which one of my teachers used to say every day. So often in life and practice, we have set ideas of how to do things or as to where knowledge comes from, we work by habits, traditions, or associations which may or may not be efficient or appropriate to the circumstances we find ourselves in.

Inspired by the motto of my teacher, I have always tried to look clearly at any situation and learn from any source, whether it be from a great famous guru/ teacher giving a lesson, or from an eight-year-old playing in the street who is telling me about their day. This approach allows you to think freely and to see things without hindrance.

With this mindset, often we find that the source of learning is unexpected and that the beginner's mind or an outside viewpoint allows for creativity or insight that someone well established within a practice or tradition doesn't have.

The power of experience and insight, however, is also of utmost importance and gives reliable, powerful and lasting benefits to our training. It is for this reason I've always sought out the opportunity to train with and spend time with people who are better at what I am seeking to achieve than me. After all, a guide who has walked the path repeatedly and gone further into the mountains is who you wish to listen to and be guided by. Sometimes by taking the time to learn from someone else who is experienced and dedicated, you can pick up on a very specific approach or way of looking at things which is a great empowerment. Often understanding an exercise or practice in the right way is what leads you to be able to connect with it fully, because we have mental blocks within us which we are unaware of until they're released.

In addition to this, I have even found that there can be a benefit to spending time with someone with a completely different approach, even one that I strongly disagree with or find objectionable. In fact, it can be very advantageous to see a very different way of thinking or doing things whether it is effective for the practitioner, or if sometimes it's in truth, holding them back

In these cases, it seems the contrast is like a light that shines upon my practice as even great masters have blind spots and we should learn from all things. After an observation like this, I know more about my approach and opinion because of my disagreement with their viewpoint or way of doing things. It makes me think about why I am doing things and how to amplify various positive effects.

Yet, there is far more potential from learning from a true Adept. When you are near someone who is a genuine master and practising the same skill, there is a lot going on beyond most people's perceptions.

Unconscious and higher learning takes place on all levels.

On the physical level, you may not know it but you are imitating small movements and adjustments to posture, and on the emotional level you match the ideal state of mind or attitude that leads to success. Mentally and spiritually your focus lifts as it takes on the same feel and vibration as your guide while your energy centres come into alignment.

While all this is taking place, our higher selves meet and are having a conversation and a lesson that is more subtle and important than anything our personalities are aware of.

This volume is an opportunity for the reader to be able to benefit from the experience of long-term dedicated genuine practitioners of the system of Franz Bardon in a similar way as I have benefited from spending time with those more advanced than myself.

It may seem that reading the words of another does not have the potential for direct transmission in the way I describe, but let us remember that from a hermetic point of view that our words are our thoughts made manifest. So when you read the words written by others, it is an opportunity to tune into their way of thinking and their approach to things. This will give you a chance to learn on all levels, including the inspired lessons by imitation and attunement mentioned earlier.

I recommend that the reader approach this book as a training manual, imagining that each interview is an opportunity to learn from an experienced practitioner in the same school as them, making notes when they find something useful and really noting the similarities between the different practitioners so as to find the golden thread of wisdom. If during your time reading this volume you find one author that you really feel in tune with, then this may be an invitation to further explore that practitioner's works.

~ Martin Faulks

PREFACE

This book was born out of the inspiration to share valuable knowledge, wisdom and insights from adepts who have worked through Franz Bardon's three books.

Falcon Books Publishing was formed as a way to assist practitioners on their hermetic path. When we began there were very few platforms available offering guidance for those working through Bardon's IIH.

We began in 2016 publishing books on these subjects and since then have grown and expanded due to the interest and support of the Franz Bardon community. At the same time, we began a series of interviews on our website, searching out adepts within this field who had already been through IIH, to share their experiences and also to offer support and advice for those still working their way through this system.

These interviews were collected from blog posts over five years, focusing on subjects that practitioners found the most challenging aspects in IIH. Due to their popularity, we decided to compile this wisdom and knowledge into one book to preserve it for future generations to come.

~ Tanya Robinson
Falcon Books Publishing

Illustration, The Magician, by Justin B

QUESTIONS & ANSWERS

Interviews with Experienced Practitioners

THE FRANZ BARDON COMMUNITY

Chapter 1: André Consciência

Introduction

André Consciência is from Portugal and has been a dedicated Bardon practitioner for twenty-one years. He joined Fraternitas Hermetica (an order based on the works of Bardon) while still a minor and had an initiator that stood even after the order vanished. He also has worked with his old initiator for twenty years. He has experience of other magical systems such as, AMORC, Order of Michael's Grail (with roots on Dion Fortune), Thelemic Golden Dawn and Astrum Argentum.

André teaches neo-shamanism and is also a playwright, poet, author, actor, founder of a publishing house including a music label attached Abismo Humano. He also founded the Theatre Company – CIA.Mefisteatro. He enjoys creative writing and is a practitioner of Chi Kung. However, Bardon's system has always been central to his practice.

He works as an artist (performer, actor with his theatre company and musician) and a published author on hermetic literature, namely a Portuguese title, *Projecto Prometeus* and the other is called *The Way of Abrahadabra* in which was intended to give the Abrahadabra formula the proper hermetic and Taoist methods and disciplines (stripping it away from the religious aspects of Thelema and all its folk rituals). Finally, he is also the head of three artistic and cultural associations.

Questions & Answers

Question 1

☉

Please you could share a little of your journey and how you came to follow Bardon's work?

André: First of all, let me thank you for the invitation. It is an honour to be among like-minded friends. I will talk about how I discovered Bardon and, hopefully, share a little of my journey in the process. I come from a family with a history of occult and spiritualism, on the one hand, and witchcraft on the other. I grew up between suspicions of my home being hexed, incorporations and possessions, with all the bad and all the good that comes with it. I soon came to realize adults around me at that time were not very aware of what was going on regarding these matters. They mostly had no clue of how to take hold and control these forces in a preventive manner. After reading Allan Kardec and joining a spiritualist centre, I realized that this philosopher didn't have the proper answer to the questions of his doctrine. I was also becoming a teenager, and the child in me was giving way to a larger spirit, which I didn't seem to be able to contain. I was awakening to a lot of theories and memories which I would try to write, draw and organize, but I was losing control. To speed up the process, I fell in love with a young student from a Wiccan coven who soon died. Wicca wasn't anywhere near to satisfy my thirst either, although I respect it, and the death my girlfriend brought opened up ahead of me as an even larger abyss of mystery. I had to take care of it. I started studying everything, from art to philosophy, to occultism, while insomnia was hitting hard under the persistent call of something unknown yet known all the while. I ended up accidentally joining a strange sect led by two people who were feeding our fantasies the best they could, only to tell us it was all a lie, in the end, except the power and wisdom we had absorbed from out of those induced fantasies. Fine, I went on, strangely stronger than before, and now I was becoming learned in theosophy, reading such works as Blavatsky and Alice Bailey, and at the same time studying the hermetic works of Aleister Crowley. Theosophy had also brought me to meet the congregations of its most dream-like states, the new agers and their close relations with the ascended masters, along with their channelled techniques. But, to summarize it, I had three priorities at the time:

1. The philosophies of Omraam Mikhael Aivanhov and the Great White Brotherhood which I still hold in great account.
2. I had a teacher; An old man I had met that claimed to be an expert concerning the ascended masters and their teachings
3. Lastly, understanding Crowley's work

I had a student although I was still a minor, an artist who always seemed to be delighted to see me and to hear me, gazing longingly. I was full of light, radiant like the Sun, in opposition to what one might expect after the death of a teenage passion, teenage passions always being of an obsessive character in at least one or another aspect. I often felt that I was full of light because I was inspired and under protection, but what if I stepped beyond that spotlight into the dark? Was I not being like what I once had come to criticize? Was that safety, that light, mine, or was I just sitting under it? Then, my initiator appeared in an esoteric discussion group. He made it seem like I was losing precious time. Crowley was confusing in his opinion, at least to the beginner, while more or less superfluous to the mature magician.

The ascended masters, under the new age perspective, were astral vampires that he had met himself, and they were wearing the masks of true masters. He gave me the book *Initiation Into Hermetics,* by Franz Bardon, and told me to read it and tell him my thoughts.

I did read it. I found it of good quality and fascinating, while the old man who claimed to be an expert on the ascended masters would tell me: 'it's fine if you want to ride a donkey when you already have a horse'. I decided to test that person who had given me the book. I told him the book was alright but had a major issue, and I asked him which element was the most important to master first. 'Fire', he replied. 'Yes, that was also my impression after reading Bardon,' said I 'but the right answer is in the water, for it is through its love that the balance of akasha comes to be, then all other elements find harmony. 'The book is flawed,' I thought to myself as being very smart upon saying it. Then he replied, 'Nonsense, what can love do without the will to learn from it or to express it? If anything, without will, love destroys character and consciousness, being as the darkness before there was any light. Will puts everything in motion, it is the word of being, and it brings forth the radiance of love, but first, you must will it. What Bardon tells you, that to obtain the perfection of success in your mystical and magical pursuits, 'you need to apply the perfect method.' At this point, I thought he was smarter and had the perfect method which I found had been missing elsewhere. I came back after three days to say to him that he was right. He answered, 'Mind your steps, though. Once you come to know Divine Providence you immediately become a pawn and a king, and if you do not get a hold of your consciousness, you will always end up in the pawn's perspective.'

I spent some time training in IIH until he introduced *Fraternitas Hermetica* to me and started to train me. But that was just the beginning of my journey, I explored many things on my own, and I was never really the standard 'white lighter.'

At each step, I would conquer and would only rest after meeting with its shadow instead of frightening it away and risking the dangers of ignorance. I think this multiplied the facets of my initiatory adventures.

Question 2

⊙

Could you share your insights of the Taoist path and how you have used it within your title The Way of Abrahadabra?

André: The Taoist methods are not as present on the *Way of Abrahadabr*a as are the hermetic methodologies, nevertheless, they are more often similar than what is generally known. For instance, the Taoists have their own practice of rising on the planes and the Celestial Masters have accounts of astral travels to distant realms in search of the divine. Tao means 'The Way,' the reason why the book was named 'The *Way of ABRAHADABRA,*' yet *The Way, or the TAO*, and *Abrahadabra* are the same, for the final dynamism of Abrahadabra is translated as 0=2,

210, or NOX. NOX is the trinity of 0 composed of the Two Columns of the Temple of Solomon, the Pentagram, and Death, the magician standing between life as expressed by the duality of the columns and the death of dissolved duality, treading on The Way, that path of non-effort called the TAO, which brings us to the original meaning of Abrahadabra and to that eternal now which states, 'I create as I speak'. This is one way of formulating magical equilibrium. It also points out, there is wisdom, love and Will unified as a single consciousness, the akasha manifests, becoming electromagnetic. Abrahadabra's number is 11, the number of the hidden sphere, while at the same time it amounts to 5+6, five being the number of the microcosmos, and six of the macrocosmos. While the hidden sphere is here as the blackness of Akasha – the union of individual and cosmic expressions and their further neutralization into zero – the state of no-mind at first presents itself as the interaction of its parts, the spiritual akashic violet that leads unto the blackness. When one examines the numbers and letters of Abrahadabra one gets the Crown, the Wand, the Cup, the Sword and, finally, the Rose and the Cross as the Pentacle. It is at the Rose and the Cross that the two become one, the one being the unveiling of the zero, so that dualism is a path to non-dualism. At *Liber Al Vel Legis* we find this passage written by Aleister Crowley:

> *None, breathed the light, faint and faery, of the stars, and two. For I am divided for love's sake, for the chance of union. The Perfect and the Perfect are one Perfect and not two; nay, are none! Nothing is a secret, a key of this law.*

There is no doubt that Abrahadabra is a formula to the Tao, and I mean to say the Tao not as a discipline or a school, but a state and a being. The method in this formula is tantric and yogic, but also firmly hermetic. The Crown refers to the dominion of the mind over the phenomena it witnesses, the Wand refers to the resulting transformation of the womb of the mind into the tongue of the spirit, Will, in a magical sense, meaning a Will that comes from the faculty of consciousness. The Cup is given by the new awareness that consciousness brings when it turns its eye into itself: it is the witnessed vacuity of mind. Through such mastery of the mind, the Sword finally aligns the individual magician with the Tao, with the Akasha in its expression of Divine Providence, and this is where the Tao is yet 'The Way.' Upon the symbol of the Rose and the Cross the individual and the cosmos merge completely to become the Tao, where the 2 and the 0 are equal. It is clear that Taoism had a great influence on

Crowley, and I learned the Tao Te Ching first from Crowley's translation of the work, as well as the I Ching.

The magician following the works of Bardon will have no problem identifying with these brief explanations about the hermetic path. In Taoism, there is a place for the deification of certain disciplined men, that is, there is a place for the divine in all the structures composing a man, his soul, his body and his mind. Their immortals are as the immortals of the IIH, the ones who have attained a level of consciousness and equilibrium far enough to survive the corrosive aspects of the cosmos, being, instead, inhabited by it. In Taoism or Daoism, there are also natural spirits and deities which help the Taoist to advance, and these methods to have the creative future flow backwards, which are, in a way, identical to the magical volt sent to the Akasha as taught by Bardon. All of this is explored in some way or another at the *Way of Abrahadabra,* yet mostly the aim of the book is to arrive at the Tao, to realize that the *Way and the Tao* are translations of one another. Ultimately, the Tao becomes an attitude, the way is the non-way, and it can be attained by any means.

I divided the book into three distinct stages:

- Firstly, for the perfection of one's inner faculties and structures.
- Secondly, for the perfection of one's outer faculties in relation to one's inner faculties.
- Thirdly, for reaching beyond the outer and, consequently, beyond the inner, so that the Akasha permeates the practitioner and Divine Providence manifests through him in the world.

Taoists also have a way of sending things into the Tao and getting things from the Tao according to the natural way – that is, in Bardonist terminology, to the Eternal Now – aiming for an endless source.

Because I do not believe oriental traditions can germinate in all their purity in the West, due to the East having silence as the most constant activity of consciousness and the West exactly the opposite, I try to push the trained consciousness beyond what it can possibly perceive, that is in this case, using tricks to cross over the threshold of attachment.

The first three stages are symbolized by LVX, meaning Light. The L is the erected phallus, and it stands for an awakening of magical will, that is, the awakening of a will that comes through magical equilibrium. The V is the open kteis, and it refers to consciousness opening to receive the cosmos and the world opening to the influence of the magician. The X aligns L and V, micro and macrocosmos, forming a higher level of magical equilibrium. And finally, there is NOX, when the magician becomes the portal and no longer has to knock on the gates of power and virtue.

Question 3

⊙

FOLLOWING THIS SUBJECT OF TAOISM, COULD YOU DISCUSS THE DIFFERENCES/SIMILARITIES IN TERMS OF THE ENERGETICS? SUCH AS THE JING-QI-SHEN MODEL, WITH THE IDEA OF TRANSFORMING ONE SUBSTANCE INTO ANOTHER, WHEREAS IN IIH WE DO NOT STORE WE JUST IMMEDIATELY USE THE ENERGY.

HOW HAVE YOU BROUGHT THESE TWO MODELS TOGETHER IN YOUR PRACTICE?

André: Interesting. I have a tale yet to be published named, *Father Moon and the Desert of Di Yu* which explores some of both. A Taoist searches for the one they called 'Father Moon,' which is said to live in a jade palace, for he thinks Father Moon is one of the Taoist immortals. But it is actually an elemental of the earth element. This passage hints at the difference between both ways of seeing the world, but it is only a superficial difference.

> I woke up in a comfortably furnished room with a jade table, several chairs and a large bookcase that covered a whole wall. Sitting at the table was Monpai, with his smooth, young face, moving at once tired and fast. "Why are you here?" He asked impatiently. I anticipated this dialogue, nevertheless a cold sweat pierced my mind. "Are you not the father of the West? And do you not hold the

> secret of eternal life and the entrance to paradise?" I asked boldly. The golden eyes on the damsel's face penetrated my spirit. "I see you're not like the others. There is purpose in you." Monpai spoke in a nervous voice, a voice which sung like the voice of a child. "But what you say about me can not be said of me alone" he concluded. "Yes… in my eastern culture there was a jade palace made by jade miners, there the Queen was a fierce goddess with tiger teeth, always ready to send plagues unto the world. But before the TAO she became benign, planting a peach tree that gave each Aeon the peach of immortality." I argued. "I see, you came for fear of death. But how will I forgive you for invading my solitude?" He gestured with thin milky arms and delicate fingers. "Immortality I grant. A peach tree I do not have." He pulled a flute from his shirt pocket. "I have a flute carved from the vertebrae of the world." At that moment I nervously searched for my TAO cross in my robes and stopped. Monpai shrugged, sensual as a lost breeze whirling in the snow. "I am not your motherly queen. I come from the period of the great formations of coal, generated in forests and exuberant marshes back then in tropical England. I've seen the seas swallow down the earth and continents become ice. I lived when on Earth there was only one Continent and the trees rose a hundred feet high in the Age of Amphibians. My flute has commanded one-meter arachnids and today commands mankind." I meditated on it all and asked, "Are you a Yaoguai? Does an animal become powerful and immortal by virtue of being worshipped?" But Monpai laughed sweetly and dangerously at me.

In the depths of its ancient and Pagan traditions, the west is wild and primal, the east is primal and gracious. But hermetism, being western, is still eastern philosophy going through a Greek filter. It is a fine place to find a balance between cultures. The Akasha in all its spectrum is ever beyond and ever-present and the way to approach it in its extensiveness is in the way of the TAO, the path of non-effort. The magician mingles with the unplanned patterns of the universe and, flowing, disappears, the gate of the Sun then opens and drops of TAO fall through, condensation. What the hermetic magician, in turn, is made of as a whole is the TAO directly connected with the primal and raw power of matter. That makes him a master over all the elements.

In hermetism, the element of light can be produced by transmission, which is the movement of electromagnetism through a body. This means that the body, material or shape should neither absorb the light nor block it. It is the essential method of the Tao and requires complete transparency as one completely flows with his environment, becoming the dance. Electromagnetic waves are a direct manifestation of the Akasha in the manifest world, and can be divided into seven forms of radiation, from the shorter and most saturated wave to the larger and most dissipated. But it can also, as in the example you give, be accumulated, and this brings me back to a story with my initiator.

At the stage in IIH when one is learning to concentrate the fluids of the elements, he said to me 'I have something quite surprising to show you.' And he showed me a Dragon Ball Z video where Songoku was becoming a super warrior, storing vitality and then turning blond, with golden energy flowing all around him permanently. 'What the Japanese are showing on television is to be your focus at this stage. It works as bodybuilding. First, you accumulate the vitality of the elements and you can only store so much, but with time you can store more and more. Eventually, if you can store enough moonlight on your astral body for the light to fall back into itself, you become the sun, and this method of transmutation is to dissipate half of your coming nightmares regarding the soul mirror as you progress".

This is not too hard to explain outside the field of fluidic condensations. If one virtue of inspiration is pushed into becoming wise, it is closer to becoming a practical power to be applied in the world. If such wisdom learns to love, it is the most effective way, and will have everything surrounding it. It finally becomes a skill and a strength, fully present in the outside world. Likewise, if the magician takes a power and soaks it in love, this power becomes magnetized, and if he so continues to bring it closer to the Tao, that loving power becoming wise and then inspired, it is no longer just a power, but a portal into the spirit realm, a door to the kingdom of light and a torch of initiation.

Bardon has also contemplated the transformation of virtues and faults on the soul mirror, but on occasion, the magician is not yet quite experienced at manipulating the fluids. Jing Qi Shen works with essence, vitality and spirit, just as hermetism works with the elements, vitality or the fluids and the Akasha. The three treasures are also moral virtues that connect the Taoist to the Akasha and its phenomenal aspects of the eternal now. In IIH, the Jing, being the qualities, is breathed in, and this is the Qi, nurturing the Shen as soul and mind and bringing it forward as the spirit or deity, while traditionally the essence is turned into the breath and the breath to spirit. This process is very similar to the process taught by Bardon on breathing qualities and vitality into the blood and from the blood into the astral and mental body. Then, traditionally, the spirit is refined into emptiness. And this is exactly also what my initiator has taught me, to use the breathing exercises to create magical volts out of myself, refining the electromagnetism that comes out of the quadripolar volt into the akasha. The Qi can also be seen as the body – mental, astral or physical – and the Shen as willpower, but in any case, all these variations are telling us the same tale, and this tale is almost omnipresent in *Initiation Into Hermetics*.

Question 4

⊙

What advice would you give to students of IIH based on your journey?

André: Act on IIH with rigour and according to its indications but think of it with intelligence. What I have come to realize is that at each step Franz Bardon is giving us elements to form a language so to speak and the rules of its grammar, but becoming fluent in a language depends on its creative use. It is said that to learn a language well, one needs to start thinking in that language. Almost any exercise at IIH can combine with any other, and this is how you begin to understand Bardon on a dynamic level. Men and women of western cultures get bored easily, they need entertainment, but there are so many ways in which you can engage with IIH as you progress that the only real reason remaining for the sincere aspirant to quit is to have a lack of imagination, and imagination also can be trained.

Most of the students I had under my supervision gave up when it came to obtaining an empty mind. Many successful magicians have noticed this issue and have made suggestions. I will add that if it is too hard, try mastering the previous exercise in many different ways. Eventually, imagine a single star in a night sky with nothing else on it. Then, remove the star. You will trick your mind into thinking you are fixing your thoughts on an image as you are used to, but what you are really doing is uniting with silence and allowing it to take over. Also, do something to learn about silence if it is lacking in you. For instance, there are cromlechs that I visit here in Portugal that will literally silence your thoughts without any effort on your part. If you fix your thoughts long enough on such landscapes while you are standing on them you will end up obtaining their qualities. Working on the soul mirror is the second reason why students quit. Those who managed through mastering their thoughts may turn their backs at this time. Nobody likes to be judged, although we judge ourselves all the time as if someone else is doing it. Try not to think of your faults as sins and things to be ashamed of. Add psychology to the disciplines and transpersonal psychology. Communicate with your vices, listen to them with active listening, let them feel understood. Encourage their passive and docile loyalty and have them never lie to you or try to trick you. Engage with your virtues as well, fix your thoughts on them and realize their dance and their elemental grace.

Virtues and strengths are not just obligations, they are muses and sources of inspiration. If you feed a virtue well enough it will eventually submit the vices under its supervision. Then comes the question of the balance between the elements. You have not only the number of qualities at each element to think about, but also the intensity of each quality. If qualities are lacking in one particular element, you can create them. Meditate on them, breathe them in and out, and eventually practice those qualities and interactions in the world during your daily life. You can start by playing the character of one who has the quality you are trying to create.

Firstly, write down the character's file of the traits the character has, what led him to have such traits, and what his ambitions are. You can even add his tastes and his appearance to enrich your imagination. When you play that character it will eventually teach you about its strengths and virtues through gnosis, that is, through knowledge that is not only intellectual but also sensorial and emotional.

Your birth chart might bring you some new clues on the subject if you are learned in astrology. You can balance the birth chart not so much by trying to erase the aspects you dislike but by filling it with balancing traits, and you will have the graphics to help you on this mission. If you are not learned in astrology or if you do not believe it, it remains that we grow up under the stigma of being of such and such sign, and we eventually adopt its traits. But we, as magicians, can balance a sign by invoking another, that is, by having another sign form inside of us that balances the first. If you manage to succeed, remember that your work concerning the soul mirror is not over nor will it ever be. I have seen those with greater training, greater experience and greater success than me eventually falter. The defect of great magicians is often pride, a blind pride, and its servant is an obsession towards control and perfection. That is why it is important to keep yourself in check, even if you now have all the tools to beat your weaknesses, you can still be deceived. After a while, it does you no good to obsess about the soul mirror constantly, and it becomes a block in itself. It is sufficient to find some form of routine. For instance, once a week breathe in the elements that constitute your magical equilibrium as shown on the soul mirror, and out your weakness. It also helps to locate the positive traits in your body and have the vitality flow between them. There are zones within the body where the tensions of the defects and vices lay. You can perform a good oily massage and dissipate such tensions by transferring your conscience to the affected muscles.

On new moons and full moons watch your thoughts, feelings and bodily impulses, and if you have crafted your magical hat as taught in PME, use it on this occasion. You will realize how most of your thoughts and feelings aren't yours but are automatic responses to automatic thoughts. Still, sometimes you might be visited by a thought that is your mission in this life, or by an emotion that connects with your soul throughout all of your lifetimes. Be that as it may, your vices and weaknesses will flee because of your divine vigilance. Yet this will also give you true authority over them. During solstices and equinoxes fix your silent concentration on the traits of the soul mirror. If your weaknesses are hiding something they will reveal it, and if your virtues have guidance to give it will be given. Finally, when the year is turning, write down a new soul mirror from the start.

By updating one's soul mirror one can keep track of what keeps coming back and whatnot. In terms of health, it is important to take note, for example, if loneliness keeps coming back again and again it might not just be a case of melancholy, but a symptom that one is not dealing correctly with how he relates to other people.

Thirdly, there is the densest form of astral travel, or, as I like to name it, the etheric projection. Where the magician has to concentrate great amounts of energy he has to let go at the same time, or he will keep coming back to the physical body. Transferring one's consciousness into the blood and projecting from out of it might help.

Question 5

⊙

How significant is the process of moving from Step 8 of IIH into PME and KTQ?

André: That depends on the goals of the magician. One can imagine the IIH as High School, the PME as University, and KTQ as a Master's Degree. High School is good enough to have you go about in the world as a working man or woman, and in this case, a man or a woman working for the manifestations of Divine Providence. Someone who has completed high school can always go to university, where he will learn many wonders that he, at least before the internet, would before the internest would not have the means to find out for himself. Believe me, the entities in PME have perspectives that we can hardly access by other means, and it takes years of exploring the spheres as learned at the IIH to find intelligences so solid and of such a high degree. Our mundane universities are full of proud and frustrated teachers, but not this one, not at this sacred university. At KTQ you learn to speak in the same language of these intelligences, your word becomes the Shekinah, the holy dwelling of Divine Providence.

That being said, I am not sure if I am truly suited to answer this question. I was presented to PME little by little as I progressed. When I trained to fix my thoughts I was given a pen and told to think of a light expressing absolute victory while gazing continuously at that pen. When I was finished the pen was shining in the dark. I was told that it was by similar methods that I would later consecrate the sword as a magical weapon. To help me through the steps I was sometimes given an intelligence of the Moon Sphere, of the zone girdling the earth, or an elemental, depending on the nature of the lessons to be obtained on that step. I was to fix my thoughts on the sigil while emptying the mind, an astral fluid would start to flow and I was to breathe it or travel on my mental and later, on my astral body to activate it. Obstacles to the soul mirror as major issues at home or the strong nightmares that kept me from sleeping year after year, etc, were pacified at the intervention of those entities and, finally, my dominion over the elements in what concerns the soul mirror was crowned by the consecration of the corresponding magical tools by the means at my disposal at that stage, although I would keep coming back to them with newly acquired methods.

I was taught to meditate in the centre of the circle and about the centre of the circle, and also about what every other magical tool given in PME was veiling. This was part of my process through IIH, but although I made fluid condensers and talismans that would connect me to the wisdom of certain elementals and certain entities of the moon sphere, I only evoked a being into the triangle on the physical at step 9. I admit I was also given some cosmic letters while perfecting my skill to concentrate the elements, so that I would know the elements' full composition and, once skilled at the akashic trance, what combinations were to connect the different elements with their akashic source, by such means keeping the process of breathing or nourishing the element going on by itself.

Moving from IIH to PME and KTQ can be significant in that neither PME nor KTQ is more of the same. They are truly an addition to IIH. Still, completing *Initiation Into Hermetics* is an award enough and, on an essential level, one will be no less without touching PME and KTQ.

Question 6

⊙

Though PME is a very private journey, is there anything you can share? Such as the beings you met, the differences between the spheres, including anything that took you by surprise?

André: Everything took me by surprise and still does. I only had five full materializations, flesh and bone. These are materializations where even if you try you cannot see past the intelligence, physically and not only physically. One was with the Greek deity Pan according to Bardon's method. The second was something near to an accident. The third, was with my guide according to Bardon's method. The fourth, with Bardon's method and N'Aton. The fifth, with an entity from Abramelin using Bardon's method.

At such a level of density Pan appeared to me as an absolute nightmare, everything froze, including my mind, but in the aftermath, he boosted the natural power of having the elementals respect me as an authority even as one of their own. This evocation changed the constitution of my body in the space of a few months, especially my legs, but all for the better.

The second time took place in a forest on the site of an abandoned monastery which I was allowed to explore. After months of working on ceremonies and on the space, having placed a grid of fluidic condensers buried beneath the ground something like a humanoid lizard, that had not been evoked, appeared. It gazed at me for ten seconds and disappeared. During that period of the experience, nature went completely silent, including elements such as the wind, and my mind instantly noticed not with the silence of the silent monkey, but the silence of no monkey at all (if you can understand the metaphor). Even my heartbeat stopped. Yet, this time I was fully present. With my guide (my Holy Guardian Angel), I dedicated a whole summer to him, and eventually, he often became fully materialized, but at the end of that time I had planned for, the operation and the instincts of my body were afflicted by an irrational eminence of death. Finally, with N'Aton, the personification of the collective consciousness of humanity as flowing from the best possible future, the operation, aiming for global change in the present, was entirely pleasant. The only strange phenomenon which occurred, when I finally left the cave, was that the mountain was on fire and emitting smoke.

Lastly, with the being from Abramelin The Mage I realized that although the psychic saturation in the air would be unbearable to almost anyone, I was totally at ease and in full dominion of my faculties. I tried full materialization only five times, and upon realizing that I had come to my own sense of perfection in the matter I left it behind so far. Most of the other evocations appeared to be in the flesh, that is why we train each sense in IIH. But if you become distracted or try to look beyond the being, the being becomes more or less holographic or eventually a presence distorting in the air. This method is fine and safer and, according to the laws of the triangle, still gives the intelligence power to act on the physical realm. For the sake of brevity, I will give one example of a frightening nature. Although, I had perfect and positive results with intelligences from Saturn. I once conducted an operation where I asked one of them to show me the root of my fear and to teach me how to deal with it. While he appeared at first in the appearance of a very fresh and very ancient holy man, he became horrendous after, and kept being horrendous until having come to the conclusion that I had obtained what I had asked for. He gave me some rules to follow in my communications with him and I also settled my own rules. He obviously never failed, but I once failed in keeping with the method and a scream like the ripping apart of the veil between the spheres was heard, one of my cats defecated and died of a heart attack, the other cat ran away to never come back. My dog, which was outside, died the next day from a similar heart attack. The intelligence would try to have me break the circle: I eventually heard a motorbike riding in through the chamber I was using, the noisy motor, the flashlight on me and someone looking as if I was doing something forbidden, but there was no way for a motorbike to get in that space and I refused to believe it. Eventually, the noise and the light went to the background of my attention and finally disappeared. After that, when I suddenly experienced a fear of something happening, it would then manifest within a short period of time. I remember fearing for no reason that the two guys in front of me at the bar would start fighting and one broke the glass on the head of the other and there was blood at my feet. Or fearing a thunderbolt would fall near me and having one fall on the house next to me in seconds, breaking its wall. Happily, the house was under construction and had no inhabitants.

This became a nihilistic period for me, it was the only time that I thought I would fail miserably. The things I believed in all started to show a different face of their own. I would sleep all day and night. But through my disbelief, I started having wonderful dreams, and one day I woke up to realize that I didn't need to believe anything, for everything was there anyway, as a timeless garden to be a part of. I felt a deep spring in me and strangely the entity assured me that was all I needed to know, and was again of a benign disposition. The next day, I dreamt of a girl, and on that day I met a girl exactly like the one in my dream. As she invited me out, I started to go out more and to live life again as natural as possible and certainly more natural than before. But, contrary to what had happened with Pan, this operation had ill effects on my legs and it took one year to recover back to full health. There are dangers on a psychological level caused by the influence over the physical plane from lesser entities.

I once worked with a negative intelligence from the sphere of the moon with the intent to get rid of my emotional delusions in a way that the rational analysis of the soul mirror wouldn't reach. For such an operation I allowed contact in dreams. The intelligence would give me prophecies during my dreams of betrayals that would come from my dear ones. They were all nonsense, yet they still happened every time right on the day that I would wake up. In my dreams, the entity would then become a clown and laugh at me, but I started to realize that the mime was like me yet dressed and painted like a mime. Eventually, after the entity had tried to give me, from her mouth, a green serpent that I hypnotized with my wand, I dreamed that I was inside the mime and looking at me as I really am, and while I had the mask it was the person's face in front of me that was an illusion. I offered that person to the cosmic void. The next day, the intelligence and I concluded that the job was done and the process was complete.

Although the entities Bardon obscures, such as the entities of Mars and Saturn or even the air elementals – sometimes cause great confusion and dispersion to the non-enlightened mind – can be hard to take on, the others have the minds of guides and, if abused, will give no harsher punishment than that of a good teacher.

The important thing to keep in mind is that the magician is no longer just a magician when evoking beings to the triangle, he is divine, charged with omnipotence, omniscience, omnipresence and immortality and keeping with his akashic trance. I also believe there are few human beings capable of abusing flesh and bone materializations without very dangerous possible side effects on the physical level. Aside from that, constant evocation, even if not as dense, may cause dependency for the magician. Not only that, it may even become like a drug that will cause him to hallucinate outside the operation, or lose contact with the human world. Thus being, most of the things one learns in the context of magical evocation are difficult to translate into the mundane human experience. At any rate, good communication with the beings in PME is made of surprises of the heart, mind and the body expanding, so one is continually surprised.

About the spheres, it may be important to notice that in IIH, Bardon walks us through the abilities they offer as seen from Malkhut. Beyond that, each sphere can be as vast as the planet Earth in terms of variation, or wider, and to limit them beyond Bardon's, or for example, William Mistele's descriptions can be fatal.

Yet, as a most imperfect guideline, I'll leave my own brief description of the spheres. The sphere of the moon teaches of that which moves mind, body and matter in terms of cycles, automatisms and self-regulation. It is the magnetism wrapping it all into a transcendent state or fluid.

Mercury is thought of as 'splendour' in the Hebraic traditions, this means that it is not entirely intellectual. A rabbi would have the student understand the Torah from the glory that emanates from its passages. And it is through the glory that the transcendence of the moon sphere becomes articulated into a system or a language to be spoken and understood. While this glory is still as a ghost, a reflection, art gives it a solid body of light which not only encloses the splendour, moreover, literally, a Holy Mass, which opens up the gates of the sun. The erotic devotion that it requires is absorbed from the sphere of Venus. The deliverance it provides brings the magician to cross the veil of illusion, the veil of Paroketh, his ego – that is, the survival instincts of his automatisms. And then he steps unafraid into the gates of the Sun, where he knows himself through all his lifetimes, past and future, and at the same time creates himself. This is the magician's individuality that was being obstructed by the "ego", it is as the electromagnetic body of his consciousness in its purest state and from this point of view the individual needs no self in order to be and to be contained. He still has to have enough willpower to put it into practice on a cosmic level, for he is now as a creative block of Divine Providence, and of such disciplines as great as to move the sun speaks the sphere of Mars.

In the Jupiter sphere, the individual attains to the double-consciousness, he is not only the individual but, simultaneously, the collective consciousness of all the sunlike beings, the company of the stars, for he has reached outside. Finally, there is Saturn, the whirlwind of destiny upon which such collectives act. Saturn is not only the sphere of limitations and their liberating initiations, it is also the sphere where these stars go to dream and to create the world anew.

Question 7

☉

Could you tell us a little more about your teacher and how it helped you progress through Bardon's works?

André: My teacher is maybe one of the most puzzling miracles that I have witnessed. He gave me a lot for many years and was never selfish or vile, not once. Such an example, he is already the greatest talismanic – in the sense that each of us is a talisman to the other – to be the help one might need. Then, he was the most creative magician that I have had the honour to meet. I do not mean that on an artistic level but speak of creativity applied to the hermetic disciplines instead. Intelligent could be a more exact term. He saw keys everywhere that I didn't, nor anyone else that I know or that I have come to read and, most surprisingly, they were the correct keys. With his help, going through IIH was not a penance that so many seem to talk about, it was probably the most engaging experience that I ever lived. Also, he knew when to vanish.

Once he vanished for three or four years, but it always felt like he was doing it at a perfect time. We often worked and meditated together, and once I had worked with him my enlarged capacities would no longer diminish. At certain stages of our progress, we became a lot like teammates, anchoring each other to potentialise our practices which we were pursuing individually before and after. If I was to speak of all he taught me, I would have to write a book, but then again, it wouldn't be my book to write. Most of all he broke down each step of IIH into several steps, since each step would benefit from the next in order to be perfected and reconstructed. This made it easier and faster, not longer and harder. It remains to say that he didn't base himself on hermetics alone, he studied the Norse traditions and the Eddas, Sufism, Ninjitsu and Taoism.

QUESTION 8\

☉

PLEASE YOU COULD SHARE WITH US MORE ABOUT THE HORUS MAAT LODGE?

André: The Horus Maat Lodge is a lodge for adepts, it does not have a training system of its own but, while accepting a myriad of traditions and its methodologies, it does have its own praxis. It focuses on the magick of Maat, as a counterweight to the explosive Horus. While Horus is a liberating light, consuming all limitations, Maat is balance and justice. Her virtue is Truth, whose power is that of constant transformation and evolution. In this paradigm Horus becomes the white globule of Maat, eliminating tyrannic structures to give truth and balance a natural space to manifest and grow. We function as a decentralized but seriously organized cyberlodge. The lodge has forty years and we have adepts from many corners of the world, divided in nexuses, and from many traditions, from Thelema to Vodoun, Wiccan priests and priestesses to Gnostic bishops, members of the Martinist orders, members of the AMORC, Chaos magicians, etc. We consider art to be magic too, for it works within its own discipline with the symbols and the invisible planes to bring change into the world, and give the solid artist the place of a rightful Adept. As stated in the Chart of the Horus Maat Lodge, we are tolerant except for intolerance and bigotry. I would say most of our ethics can be summarized at *Priesthood: Parameters and Responsibilities*, by Nema. A common inspirational book is *Liber Pennae Praenumbra,* where Nema channels Maat and describes her visions, revealing N'Aton as a possible healthy future for the planet, he representing the double consciousness of the sovereign individual who is fully telepathic and empathic, the reunion of every human being in such a state being the evolution of the species. This is an evolution where nuclear warfare or warfare of any kind will not be possible. Where through the collective consciousness as accessed by the individual, everyone will be able to feel and communicate with Gaia – meaning nature, the earthzone and the elemental kingdoms – as well as to understand the intelligences of other planetary spheres and constellations. Thus, the environment will be safe. Our aim is to become talismans that preserve and offer a greater potential for this kind of change.

Our magical word is IPSOS; meaning "by the same mouth" and, in my understanding it implies, among other things, an instant balance between the inner and the outer, is that our words and actions towards others are also swallowed/suffered by us, the reason why it would not make sense to commit injustices and lies. The works of Nema herself seem to give particular importance to the Tao through the dancing of the masks and the black flame, the purifying flame of the empty mind. The dancing of the masks implies also the practice of ascending in the planes: that is, when your vision and understanding becomes obstructed on a plane you rise to a higher level and start perceiving and acting through it. The levels are disposed through the Tree of Life and are similar to the astrological planetary spheres described by Bardon. Dancing the masks also implies that to bring truth into the hearts of the many we come to meet in life one has to become 'the truth' in many languages. On an ultimate level, it is the black flame, the empty mind turned into a fluidic and dynamic element, that is masked by its elasticity to take on different forms and to reflect the truth.

Question 9

☉

Regarding working through IIH which aspects did you find the most challenging and why?

André: While I did ascend in a spiral to meet with my guide as taught by Bardon, this was not my first close encounter with him. I followed the procedures that were given by the Fraternis Hermetica whereby, using a certain method, you meet with a personification-plasmification of your own astral substance, or better yet, something between your astral substance and the 'Soul of the World' as put by Giordano Bruno. This personification is knowledge itself and takes many forms and guises. It is only after you get it under perfect control and out of the way that the guide will appear crystal clear, as if one had removed the scales from one's eyes. While there are some valid methods given by adepts from the school of Franz Bardon to check whether the intelligences or elementals being contacted are real or products of the imagination, they are never bulletproof.

Many of the beings that I met while working with the Tatwas were just this plasmification that stands as a bubble between one's self and the world. I started running through my magical diaries from years past and the number of such cases started to grow page by page.

Question 10

⊙

"The real challenge is truly knowing something. We are trained to manipulate mind, body, the soul and the senses into some form of hypnosis that allows us to cross the bypass that binds us to the most mundane realities."

Please could you explain this in more detail?

Andre: Eliphas Levi, *The History of Magic*, in a way seems to turn against the truth of magic, exposing the fevers of astral intoxication and its final products of hallucination and self-deceit. He tells us that the astral light is the devil himself. Aleister Crowley tells of a great number of self-claimed adepts who are but neophytes blinded by the shining images of the moonlight, he considers the phenomenal world not that important altogether only to fall into a greater pit, the abyss of the void and its non-phenomenal hallucinations.

It is no wonder that, at Crowley's tradition, in the matter of validating some sort of absolute truth, the paradox that resolves the problems of magic is in Kether then, or at the grade of Ipissimus.

When the magician reaches the highest form of himself he is just a simple man and no more. In *The Way of Abrahadabra* I close the book by telling the reader that, if he has gone through all the exercises, he has experienced so much that he can finally remain at peace again as a simple, mortal man. The great worm of hell formed out of curiosity will no longer blind him and attack him with fever and delirium. Goodness, he has earned being a common man for the first time in his life now. While I feared this kind of conclusion for the whole of my journey, I rejoice in it today. As a consolation for the doubtful pilgrim who is walking on his path, remember that the most important thing is not how absolutely real in all perspectives something is, but if it works and the proof of success: ultimately, you become a better person. Aside from that, with a teacher or without, until you become mature not only as a magician but as a regular person with a body that keeps changing until it dies, this is a very lonesome path, and it gets lonelier as you progress. An important part of your life and your identity becomes unpronounceable. This can only be counterbalanced by something Nema said "the hard work is in polishing one's perceptions. This is why I say that 90% of Magick is trash-removal", or, as an ex-girlfriend of mine from a druidic order put: "I dream of becoming a human. There is just a handful. Most of the people tend to think of themselves as divine."

Question 11

⊙

Some practitioners attempt to work with Bardon's second and third books before finishing IIH, is there a danger in doing this?

André: Firstly, if you have no knowledge and no power it's all just childs play. Playing is good for your health, they say. But if you do have some power and knowledge, once you have come to a fair amount of dominion over the elements there is no danger in working with the magical tools, but they are at their best once the magician has trained with the four divine qualities. For the circle, while it can not hurt, it is at its best once akashic trance is mastered. The hat is best used when the magician has control over his mind and his mind has become a beacon of light through the workings of silence. The triangle makes sense after the magician has learned to master his body and his hold of his situation in physical life, as well as in the mental sphere and in astral projection. It makes sense to use the lamp after having mastered clairvoyance, the incense after having clairalience, etc.

The danger is that if the magician uses these weapons before mastering what they represent it will be harder for him to believe in their strength. But depending on the magician and his level of influence over the astral fluids etc, the weapons can work the other way around, solidifying the capacities he has been searching for. Once the soul expands it does not contract, the old labyrinths, once solved, don't return to being labyrinths. Concerning the intelligences, there is no danger in using some source of inspiration. But if the magician tries to put them in the triangle before he is prepared, or has learned the proper methods, meditations and obtained magical equilibrium, he will probably be working with the densification of astral light. If the magician's concentration on virtue is not irrepressible, he will probably harbour astral larvae. He won't die specifically from it, since to be under the dominion of astral larvae one just has to wish for it, no magic is required. It is preferred that, unless the magician has a teacher, he would refrain from using PME altogether until reaching the proper step in IIH.

Above all, if he must use it and he has the skill to actually succeed in obtaining more than a pipe dream, he is most firmly to stick to intelligences of the Earth Girdling Zone – avoiding the monarchs – and some intelligences of the sphere of the moon. Bardon's intelligences are, as I said, mostly guides of a gracious nature, but even ballet being gracious, can damage the tissues of the untrained dancer if he pushes too hard or tries to go beyond his ability. For instance, a talented beginner using intelligences from the sun sphere will have little chance of succeeding, at least without lowering the vibration of the being substantially. But if by some miracle he was to succeed with strength and dignity, he would find his ego shattered instead of asleep, leading to different breeds of psychosis.

KTQ, in my opinion, has no dangers at all. Most people are capacitated to think in abstract terms, in symbolic terms, and on an emotional level. They are less able to think with the body and, because of it, won't be able to obtain the powers from the letters, only the virtues. The cosmic letters will come to the practitioner to the extent of his maturity, no less and no more, but, just as with regular meditation, they can help anyone progress. The untrained person can try then to articulate the letters between many combinations and yet unless he is a skilled philosopher of sorts, an artist, a poet, or maybe a programmer he is to do it to absolutely no avail.

Still, I once met an oriental master who told me KTQ should proceed to IIH, since the magician would have fixed all the necessary virtues even before starting the work of IIH. Although I have hinted at some potential dangers and mistakes, one is to avoid fear, remember that esotericism protects itself from harming the fool exactly by being incomprehensible to him.

Question 12

⊙

For someone who is untrained using the Tripolar method. How effective is KTQ and can it cause harm if practitioners have not completed IIH?

André: Just as the West uses yoga mostly as gymnastics and makes it ingenious, so would the practice of KTQ be to the innocent or untrained, no more than some periodic mental exercising and emotional relief.

Question 13

⊙

Some training systems could be perceived as unbalanced due to the focus being on seeking answers outside of ourselves rather than through personal development. In your experience working within occult circles have you found this to be the case?

André: I haven't found this particular problem in the Bardon tradition yet except for a grand initiator having the students strengthen their vices in order to make it a matter of life and death – as I consider our relationship with our defects is a neverending story, it doesn't make a lot of sense to me unless you want to be a rock star. Nevertheless, this picture you just painted seems to be the most common case in many other paradigms.

Depending on the context, you either have initiators imposing themselves and vampirizing their students, or the students obsessing about their "gurus". In the first scenario, you have claims of sexual abuse at *Ordo Templi Orienti*s and, with the rise of the alternative right at the *Astrum Argentum*, which was originally built to prevent communication between students and adepts in order to avoid abuse of authority, you have at some structures an almost military paradigm, coming from initiators that don't even know how a pentacle can be built and have ascended through the grades out of political strategy and that are, at best, intellectuals. I know cases in some masonic lodges where the initiators brag of having had their probationers urinate themselves during rites of initiation. After bragging to anyone willing to listen, they have a good laugh.

It also works the other way around. At a certain time in my life, I worked at a centre for alternative and holistic therapies. I had many male students humiliate themselves before me, at my displeasure, and the more I told them to be sovereign and whole, to stay standing even before the face of death the more they would bow like creeping vampires. This led me to abandon them eventually. Female students would often "fall in love" and try all sorts of seductive moves. These are the "spiritual tourists' who come to you because they want some exotic experience of surrender. If I was Charles Manson, they would surrender just the same and end up doing God knows what just for the thrill. In the best-case scenario, they eventually get bored or satisfy their touristic drive for adventure and leave by their own accord.

In another episode, I came to learn with a shaman from an Amazonian tribe. I went with a group of other caucasian men and women. As we would work with substances like Ayahuasca, Peyote and San Pedro, some of the members of the group started to become obsessed with the idea that they had to prove themselves to the shaman, for the shaman's personality was very strong and his gaze seemed to know all. Ayahuasca would then always reveal this unbalance which was a sort of aggressive shame. The shaman did everything in his power to drive those members away, begging them to take a breath and come back under another state of mind or move on with their lives, yet they kept coming, thinking they had to prove themselves harder than ever. One eventually tried to pull off his face and the shaman had to knock him out. This is the last I heard of the group.

What seems most surprising is when you have sects of actually trained adepts who turn their eyes to political power and cultural monopoly. They no longer remember their cause. They just want everything and are willing to destroy anyone to get it, like dragons sitting over a useless mountain of treasures. I was pursued by such sects, life threats included.

Well…The occult is a vast abyss. You can learn to build your divine lamp and make a star, become a sun, or you can stumble in the dark for adrenaline. The world is dangerous, and with most occult organizations the blind leading the blind the best they can. Hermetic wisdom has become a source of inspiration, but its actual laws are out of fashion. The consequence is that the occultist joins not only ignorance in its either devotional or rebellious choirs, but also its expressive side, stupidity, to the detriment of what human enlightenment there is left.

Many of these unbalanced paths can still hold some mysteries that a well-trained magician, under the guidance of magical equilibrium can "steal" for himself and, beyond that one has to understand that a lot of traditions are solely for adepts or else for certain cultures and genetic strains, I have never heard of Indians having trouble with Ayahuasca because certain tribes, grow up with it, generation after generation and use it as medicinal water.

Question 14

⊙

How important was soul mirror training regarding your own path and what approaches did you find to be the most effective?

André: The soul mirror can have its own shadow, its name is restriction and, with time, it becomes a magical blockage itself. This can happen especially if the magician has not learned to think in equilibrium.
When I talk of thinking I am not referring solely to the mind, for I usually say that each body has its own head. I, more or less, speak of this at *The Way of ABRAHADABRA*, and might as well cite it, if you would be so kind as to bear with me:

> *The Pentagram stands not only for the primal elements as we have come to learn them from the Greeks as it stands for the perfection of men in that it represents the right disposition of his parts, either they be his physical,*

> *emotional, intellectual, imaginational or spiritual components. The figure radiates the perfect equilibrium of a human being. The Pentagram also stands for the number 5, Mars, the God in Motion, and motion implies unbalance. And this, in turn implies that the absolute can only move and become something by the balance of men, his elements being in a state of perfect love in regards to one another and that harmony flowing through the perfected art of Conscious Will, for from the point of view of the absolute even harmony is unbalanced, while from our point of view, the order is our bridge to divinity. The pentagram also ensures by an equal proportion of its parts that there is no element missing or too much of an element, for such a case is the fountain of disease in whatever plane it may occur.*

We learn to use, in this grade, the scale of 4 and its balance in the 5. Although at the macrocosmos the 4 stands for the 4 states of matter: solid, liquid, gas and energy, and the 5 is the cosmos, on the consciousness of men, or at the passive centres of activity in the brain, the 4 is instinct, cognition, memory and intuition, and the 5 which results from the balance of the 4, because the balance will move consciousness forward while unbalance will keep it moving in circles. While 5, being the spirit or the akasha, once generated, stands for itself and commands the 4 by introversion, the 4, by extroversion, make up the constitution of the 4 planes to which men are restricted, by them the physical, the etheric, the astral and the mental.

Another key may be applied in which the 4 is multiplied by the 3, the 3 being intellect, emotion and the conjunction of the 5 senses which is as the reflection of the number 5 on a physical dimension. This key sets cognition, intuition, instinct and memory on each of the 3, making it 12 and, by consequence, forming the signs of the zodiac. If the magician was to follow in the presented direction of thought he would have the following analogies:

The world of the senses would have Aries as instinct, Taurus as memory, the Gemini as cognition, Libra as intuition. This would mean that the instinct to react is at the core of our senses, while the instinct to persevere in their memory, their cognition comes through duality and their intuition through harmony.

The world of emotions would have Cancer as instinct, Leo as memory, Virgo as cognition and Scorpio as intuition. In turn, this would mean that the instinct to feel is rooted in the Will to connect, our emotional memory is rooted in our sense of individuality, and that our feelings come to awareness by a search for well-being just as our emotional intuition, having no logic to be based upon, builds on the need to test.

The world of thoughts would have Sagittarius as instinct, Capricorn as memory, Aquarius as cognition and Pisces as intuition. In that context, the intellect would have an adventure as its instinct, structure as its memory, innovation as its cognition and imagination as its intuition. Even though we are still introducing this grade, the magician or future magician is to take from it his first test on mnemonics, the art of magical memory. He is to meditate on this table of correspondences until it becomes perfectly natural to him. But, although the cunning practitioner will be able to use the previous analogies during our path to adepthood, the author himself will not be applying them in the methods to be taught. This is not to take the importance out of memorizing this table, for unless the magician memorizes it in such a way that it becomes intuitive, he knows it by instinct and it moulds his perceptions. The magician will find a missing link on his magical chain or at his magical structure, and his operations are hardly going to succeed. In addition, by learning his mnemonics the magician will become naturally apt to work the correspondences to come during his exercises.

Now let us examine the pentagram further concerning the elements; on the left, we have air on the top, and earth on the bottom. On the right, we have water, at the top and fire at the bottom. The right column is the column of force and on the left, is the column of matter. Force is condensed at the heavens as water, to descend it must become pure energy, fire. Matter is condensed on earth and to ascend it must become subtler in the form of air. Now, earth and air do not influence each other directly, their vertices do not touch at the pentagram, just as water and fire do not touch. Instead, fire and air influence each other mutually, just as air and water, water and earth. Air and water influence two elements each, but fire and earth influence only one other element, for one is the densest and the other the purest. Such a diagram shows that force and matter are mutually dependent to achieve their most sublimated states, but the densest state of force can influence both its purest state and the finest kinds of matter, just as sublimated matter can influence the most condensed forms of force and the grosser kinds of form. Akasha, or the spirit, is in direct contact with fire and earth, so that it is equally rooted in the densest and in the finest modes of existence. This means that left of himself, without the secret of wisdom, man is only able to touch the divine as he experiences extremes.

To understand it in human terms, as this grade concerns the microcosm rather than the macrocosm, we would have to say that the spirit touches the senses directly and the will of the regular men, while that very same will is able to conduct the mind and can be hypnotized by it and the senses are able to reproduce feelings, or be caused by them. Emotions, in turn, can also cause thought patterns while these very same patterns can reproduce emotions back. The realm of thoughts and the reign of feelings are cyclic and circular, but the Will and the senses are, outside the realms of spirit, what men can most rely on. This means that we have attributed will to fire, thoughts to air, emotions and feelings to water, the 5 senses to the earth. Or, roughly speaking, to the fire the analogies of heat and the concentric forces, to the air the analogies of openness and lightness, to the water the analogies of fluidness and coldness, and to the earth the analogies of everything solid, heavy and rooted.

The elements move by accumulation. For instance, there was heat on the face of our planet, and that counts as one magical element, it is, therefore, the first element - from heat and the atmosphere came the winds, and the winds are the second element. We say these elements are magical because they are animated, and consequently the first and second sources of animism. From the heat, the atmosphere and the wind do the waters awaken to start their tides, and the waters are the third element. Apart from the earth being moulded by them, from the heat, the atmosphere, the wind and the tides the earth is awakened by genetic life! This is the fourth element.

And where there is conscious life there is that which we may call the aura of a planet, its astral trail, an electromagnetic field that suspends time and space around its source, and that is the fifth element. In this key, the atmosphere represents the zero, the circle around the pentagram. Another way to say this is that the will shone on consciousness and that from the interaction of the two the mind itself was born.

There was dormant energy that was moved by the interaction of the 3, and there formed the emotions. Finally, the will, consciousness, mind and emotion come to fill the centre of the body and breathe life into it.

The magician may take the time to memorize these correspondences before he goes on reading. Now one can position any attribute at each of the elements, given that the akasha remains untouched and the proper filtration is applied at the other elements. Let us choose four random qualities. We put force at the place of the earth, we place brightness at the place of the water, darkness at the place of the air and matter at the place of fire. To fire, matter is destruction or rather its material form is destructive. To air, darkness is ignorance. To water, brightness is fascination and to earth, the force is work. Now, this can be easily translated into one of the following ways:

Destruction leads to ignorance, ignorance to fascination, and fascination to slavery. Or, the slave starts to regain his individuality through fascination, and by the curiosity it evokes he recognizes his ignorance in order to destroy his chains. The Pentagram is actually the sign of the free man, for the magician who has learned to meditate properly on this diagram understands that nothing is a dead end and that every flow can be directed and redirected on the focus of his choices.

Still, the magician's work is not the same as the work of the regular individual. The magician's job is to find magical equilibrium, so when the will, mind, feelings and senses all work as one, the spirit, which is placed at the top of the pentagram, and is reproduced as the quintessence at its centre, leaving every element in touch with one another as well as with the divine.

To illustrate further. The reader may find that the four qualities we have attached to the elements form by their natural flow within the above sentences. The keyword to the sentence shown above is freedom/slavery, for neither freedom nor slavery was placed in the elements but they are the meaning we can extract from the position of their given attributes. Freedom/slavery is a dualistic keyword, just as it is dualistic for the spirit to be attached to fire and water. While a regular man may think of freedom, they think of it in terms of ascending to freedom or of losing freedom. However to the magician he perceives he is at that spot in the centre of the pentagram. In fire position he would place light, in the air he would place liberty, in the water position he would place love and, for earth, he would place life. So, from life, he would come to love, from love to liberty and from liberty to light. Such as, from light to liberty, from liberty to love and from love to life. All the attributes are in harmony and a quintessential part of each other, and this happens because the qualities are directly connected to the elements they were given and are at their original source.

Surely, we could change the scale of the keyword and still keep our magical equilibrium. If we change the scale of freedom to its grade in the fire, the spiritual word or keyword becomes light. Its focus is on the fire element, the direction in the air element, devotion in the water element and victory in the earth element. We could go on forever and not lose elemental balance and magical equilibrium. By this, we illustrate what it is to think, act and live with magical equilibrium at one's side.

Through such means, the magician can more easily move in many directions and explore without losing his magical balance. But, I was eager to explore even though I suffered slightly from restriction before I had the idea of the key to express the most vibrant virtues, one has sometimes to play and dance and wearing heavy armour won't do for such occasions.

Then there is the soul mirror which I have found to be the best device for introspection. Far inserted within a magical system, the application of philosophy is not an exact science. It takes practice for one to understand that sometimes too much of a certain quality creates weakness and some weaknesses were strengths that we were afraid to acknowledge. For instance, psychology tells us that anger is the first step to healing, so, what can we make of it? To work with the soul mirror one has to apply sensibility, intelligence and wisdom, otherwise one may end up becoming repressed by it instead. Exercising such virtues should be a warm up for the bellic (a warlike) approach that may be required of us from the soul mirror work. Some left-hand traditions speak of a 'natural way,' and that the body, if left to itself, knows its balance and a way to bring mental and emotional harmony. While Aleister Crowley, a man with a right and a left-hand formed in psychology, might have had – or not – the ability to do this successfully to call himself the solar beast. Whereas most magicians from the left-hand path don't have a single clue about how this can be done. While Anton LaVey, smart as he may have been, spoke of "indulgence instead of abstinence," indulgence itself solves nothing of the origin of human unbalance. Psychology tells us that pathologies come from fragmentation. In order to protect themselves from fracturing as a wholesome part of the psyche, when faced with trauma, they are separated from their memory and the memory, in turn, tries to assimilate them back by associating them with other phenomenal objects of the mind. Just as the fibres of a muscle, when wrongly entwined, cause pain, limitations and unbalance on the body, so do the fibres of the mind. By acting, a body tries to escape an unbalanced mind, but it is like a lost animal on an artificial labyrinth. The mind must clear, so that the beast might find its proper forest and take good care of the mind. Between the body and the mind, the astral is important, that is why exercise and conscious breath come in handy. The astral fluids have emotional intelligence and, by default, are not trapped by the body, nor by the mind: like the nature of water, they seek balance and answer to intuition.

Question 15

☉

What would you say about this statement 'Our outward success in life is a reflection of the inward success of our practice.' and axiom-As Above So Below?'

André: Ah! But there are two sentences there, surely connected but maybe not the same. About the first sentence, I would say that it is mostly correct, although maybe not entirely correct at the present level of human evolution.

While our work upon ourselves surely moulds most of the things around us or how they interact with us, some of it doesn't reach outside. There could be two reasons for this, one being that the universe, by its nature, only reacts to us to a certain extent, and the other being that there is so much of us that we do not know, that these parts are left out and so the outer seems to act partially of its own accord.

To the second sentence now: I met a very wise Christian poet and philosopher. He used to tell me that "as above, so below" is not the same as "as below, so above." He believed that heaven would only open of its own accord. To him, gnostics and hermetic magicians believed otherwise, in that they thought they could manipulate the process, building their babel tower, and for that alone, they had already corrupted the experience. To him, heaven was a gift, not something one conquers. I don't have any smart argument to overthrow him, just that the hexagram stops midway. When we earn at least paradise, then heaven descends of its own accord or, truly deserving something always comes with a surprise, a miracle factor, and that is the element of the soul-expanding, the heart that beats without asking for permission: we just have to live and organize our lives.

Organizing life: Giordano Bruno tells us that if we change the stars then we change the Earth. He did this job as a magician. The concept was that by changing the archetypes one can program the reality of the world at large. Now, this was a man living down on earth changing heaven above to change the earth below. He, as a Christian monk and later a Hermetic magician and philosopher, would still agree with my friend the Christian poet but did already outsmart him. And, by principle, Bruno and I would agree with you, that the inner connects above, and the outer below. But he and I would then open our eyes as wide as there is light and darkness and look outside at the Soul of the World in all its vastness. Eventually, we would see heaven alone, heaven and the adorer. Alas, esoteric tradition shows a strike of light upon the tower of babel and the holy flames thereof.

Now, while what I just said would make a fine closing line, this unity of two presented, what if we acknowledge yet that maybe the sentences at the question form up a single quadripolar magnet composed of Above, Below, Inner and Outer, whose electromagnetic force is as invocation/evocation? Again, I cite a small passage from *The Way of Abrahadabra*, a charade that aims to bring insight into a unity of four, and hints at a level not directly talked about by Bardon in that true vigilance is beyond the conscious and the subconscious/unconscious. While at first the conscious is spoken as a tool against the unconscious or the subconscious, it is still a reaction to the subconscious/unconscious, therefore impulsive and reactive. But in IIH the magician actually starts to work with the four divine qualities, there is no way for reason alone to grasp them.

A Charade for the Magnetic Mars, Sphere of Eternal Renovation

Invocation

A star falls as a seed
And rises as a tree of life
Now the dead will rise to greet
A sky most bright.

Evocation

My name is
The Star Sapphire,
I was about to write
"Evoked action."

This number is 4876,
We were with you from the beginning to get to the other side.

In the first poem, a star, which refers to an original life force or a cause – is invoked unto the magician and his channels are activated while his light scales up renewing his body. The lore here implies also that everything is in connection with our inner structures may be born again in its image. It is about the act of renewal that starts from the inside out and makes the magician a portal of magic and creation. While the second poem has a different source. In Jewish mysticism, sapphire, is the colour of heaven and always stands for celestial structures, supernal energy and divine knowledge. In the poem, the poet is about to write "evoked action," so that he evokes the action of writing and the poem thereof. But he tells us his name is the star sapphire, implying that his action comes from the heavenly realm of causes. When an action comes from the dimension of original cause rather than from a reactive point of view, it brings with it eternal renovation, so that through it the initiate of this sphere is to be recognized.

Question 16

⊙

Please could you tell us about your next title: Through the Soul Mirror to the Sphere of the Sun?

André: You will see news on *Through the Soul Mirror to the Sphere of the Sun*, and it will make the soul mirror itself a dynamic system of initiation into magic and mysticism. It may have the guidance of the heads of the sun, and the mission to have the magician connect directly with the source of all virtues.

Question 17

⊙

Is there anything else you would like to add?

André: I would like to add that the writings of William Mistele were of great help and inspiration while I was completing IIH. Homage to him, who is an author at Falcon Books. I will also add that I am reviewing the book following, *The Way of Abrahadabra*, and one of its missions is to address modern science in the light of magic. I feel that magic stopped at the Renaissance, and even then, it drank from Ancient Greece and Ancient Egypt. We have come to learn so much since then, and to read so many new pages on that *Book of Isis called Nature*.

Why is it that magic didn't follow? While some Chaos magicians and some Maatian magicians draw from quantum mechanics, how did we come from Ancient Greece directly to quantum science?
What of everything else that is in between?

Chapter 2: Crystalf Maibach

Introduction

Crystalf Maibach is a long term Franz Bardon practitioner. He began the work of conscious self-transformation some thirty years ago, and is active in Bardon's Opus and other hermetic and magical traditions and has been now for nearly twenty years.

Besides Bardons Work of self-transformation, his main focus lies in laboratory alchemy.

He holds a master's degree in History and has written several articles concerning mainly Alchemy and Theurgy in different magazines.

Crystalf also has a successful Blog named *Hermetic Science*[1] which covers various subjects ranging from, Franz Bardon, Alchemy, Astrology, Magic and Quabbalah.

[1] http://hermeticscience.de/

Questions & Answers

Question 1

⊙

Please could share with us a bit of your background and how you came to practice Franz Bardon's work?

Crystalf: Thank you for giving me this opportunity to share some of my experiences, gained from walking my path.

For me, it is always an interesting question, how I came to practice Bardon's work. There are so many inspirations that depending on my mood and time, different ones come primarily to my mind. So let's think about, which one I want to focus on.

I remember some of them are more dominant like (clearly) Bardon's book itself, others more reluctant. But all of them are part of my desire to grow beyond my mundane capabilities. Maybe the earliest memory I can remember of, that has something to do with personal growth is … Luke Skywalker!? Honestly, some of my earliest memories about the desire to grow in self-improvement was, when I was around seven years old and watched Star Wars for the first time. I was deeply impressed with Luke trying to become a Jedi Knight, to grow from a mere farmer boy towards being a "wise warrior" like Obi-Wan. Just like every little boy, I loved warriors, but since then I could not get along with the pure muscle types; there had to be more, the wisdom to know why and when to fight for what, just like "Old Ben." This memory was probably part of my subconscious desires when I started my quest – I think this triggered something; there was a spark that got alighted. Well, around three years later I started training in the martial art, Shaolin Kung Fu. Perhaps to learn to fight better, but what I learned was not to fight, but to control myself – my body and mind. This was the first conscious step toward transformation. Of course, I got in contact with the so-called "youth occultism" in the mid-90s also, but it did not impress me in the slightest;

in fact, I was more repelled by its egomaniac self-centeredness. And honestly, even as a fourteen-year-old I could not grasp why making a wand should give me magical powers. The magic had to come from me, not the wand. So I concentrated on school.

The first real act of magic I did with around twenty-one. I had a bad argument with a person very dear to me – and I won the argument. Sure, I won, but I hurt her with my words, my anger…and when I came home, it became crystal-clear to me that this wasn't the kind of person I wanted to be. So I decided to change myself, to develop into a person I feel comfortable with looking into the mirror. This conscious decision – without books, Bardon or rituals; it was the most magical act I had done so far.

A year later I stumbled upon IIH and found it immediately the perfect tool to reach this goal. IIH appeared from the very first moment as a systematic system of self-development, including magic – all the myths inherent still in my (the human?) consciousness, but without the tam-tam found in many modern systems of occultism. It appeared to me nearly scientific in its systematic approach, but nonetheless all about the individual. And it had no dogma! After I began the work I did in fact gain experiences in a lot of other occult systems and initiations, but after a while, I realized that none of them really gave me a lasting feeling of maturity. Sometimes even quite the opposite. So after a few years, I quit with the other stuff and concentrated on IIH, restarting in the process and since then I walk the Hermetic path. And I am still on that journey to transform myself. Still struggling from time to time, but walking on step by step. In my experience, it is not important to be perfect, but never to stop walking. Then the goal will be reached in time…

Question 2

⊙

There is a potential for practitioners to be 'stuck' for a long time on Step 1. Why do you think this is and what advice would you offer?

Crystalf: That is a tough question if every argument for getting "stuck" I have heard so far should be considered. But I think the main reason is, that most people don't really *want* to walk the Path. In truth they want other things such as, fame, love, respect and power in some way or another; these are the main reasons I deducted. And to transform their body, spirit and mind appear for them more mandatory, than an act worth of itself. So they more or less "torment" themselves with IIH and the exercises of Step 1 – and torment is no fun. Sometimes they even realize somewhere in themselves, that there is a treasure to be found in IIH, but still, they care more about other things – like sleeping an hour more in the morning. And to wake up earlier is no fun for them. But IIH should be FUN, it should be fun to change yourself for the better. And every step has its own fun.

Too often I talk to people who long to be in Step 5 or 6 because they expect some cool stuff there. But honestly guys – when you arrive there, all the stuff you do and experience appears as nothing special anymore, Such as, to project elements, just the natural outcome of your maturity. And as long as the student finds no fun in Step 1, he won't progress. Still, my favourite exercise in the whole of the three books is thought-observation! I simply love it!!! It is the foundation for everything else and teaches me every day more about me, my behaviour, my being. It is THE exercise that makes "know thyself!" possible…And all the other reasons why people don't progress are logical consequences of this subconscious unwillingness: for example, having no time is "not making time". If the student really wants to do the exercises they will be able to find the time. These arguments are following several other excuses.

Another main reason is a prejudiced approach to the exercises. Many students think they already know what Bardon is talking about and thus they don't really do *his* exercises, but the exercises they think they should do. Especially with VOM many, many, many people confuse it with Dharana or even Samadhi. That is wrong! It is not VOM, and Bardon's descriptions are very accurate. It is not "not-thinking." It is a form of concentration, the logical consequence of the other three exercises the student did before in Step 1. Thus it is concentration, like in the exercise before; the student simply concentrates on an empty "space" in their mind. They ignore the upcoming thoughts and don't get attached to them. However, the thoughts will come up as a natural process of the mind, but that is not what the student stays focused on. They stay focused on the empty space; they reject to get attached to the upcoming thought fragments. Over time, other thoughts simply disappear from the consciousness, et voilà... VOM. The best thing for aspiring magicians is to forget what they have learned so far and read and practice IIH with an open mind.

Question 3

⊙

On the subject of Step 1 and VOM,

We know this is so important but what does it bring to IIH?

Crystalf: VOM is essential to becoming capable of concentrating properly, to be open to impressions outside of ourselves. We human beings tend to perceive, what we expect to perceive. VOM helps the mind to be not attached to our expectations, thus being able to i.e. visualize the perceived form in Step 2 correctly and not only the form how we think it is. Later on the Path, we need it for depth-point meditation, then for clairvoyance as the "seen" impressions come up in our mind, and as long we are busy with our thoughts we would simply miss the messages from beyond. It is the same thing with Evocation. Human beings have no "magical powers" because mostly we are too self-centred, even too arrogant to realize there is more than we think it is in this universe. VOM helps with that immensely. Also without VOM, there is no Mental Wandering, as we get lost in the world of our thoughts and many more things.

Question 4

⊙

Please could share with us the importance of focusing on self-development along with working through the steps in IIH.

Crystalf: Why "along"??? All the steps of IIH *are* self-development! That is what it is all about. IIH is not about learning powers but becoming more yourself. To become what you *should* be. What you should be in your life. What you should be in society. Maybe even as divine as we should be. I quote Virgil from his excellent book, *The Spirit of Magic: Rediscovering the Heart of Our Sacred Art* (Second Edition).

"Magic is an act, "....to live a blessed life and to be a blessing to society. Nonetheless, there are "magical powers, of course, but… and this "but" is a BIG "but"….The funny thing is: the student will get magical powers along the way, but when the time comes when they get them, these "powers" will be of no more special significance to them. It is more like a baby learning to walk: first, it feels great, but what special significance walking has walking for even a four-year-old or even a grown-up? It simply becomes part of your being…

Question 5

⊙

What other strategies did you employ other than working on the soul mirrors to assist in further growth?

Crystalf: Awareness!

Always being aware of what is happening in yourself. Radical Self-Honesty, thus developing the ability to say "Sorry!" Everybody does make mistakes. And as long as the student is not capable of avoiding mistakes, they should at least be able to overcome their pride and say "Sorry!" But on the other hand, they shouldn't give too much to the opinion of others. The other human beings surrounding the student are also too attached to their expectations, but this is not relevant for the student. It is their expectations, ethics and maturity that matters. So forming an ideal of myself helped me a lot in my growth – like the Jedi-idea I formulated at the beginning. Make yourself a picture, a symbol of what you want to be, be it a good teacher, a good parent or maybe a kind wizard or a wise Jedi. This picture is your private symbol; it might be a fantasy, but it can help you to visualize something, to give a clear picture of what the student wants. "Self-development" or "personal growth" tend to be too abstract to be appealing over the long years of the training, especially if your life becomes a mess. Also, it helps to do some complex sports like martial arts to get in control of your body. It is not important to get a black belt but to grow in the possibilities that your body gives you.

Question 6

☉

How can we know we are truly achieving the goal of that step such as with vital force?

Crystalf: By working through the first exercise of Step 1 thoroughly. By observing your thoughts, you become used to observing yourself. By knowing exactly what is going on in your mind, you´ll simply be sure, if you are fooling yourself or if you have truly achieved something. The practice of Step 1 develops the approach towards radical self-honesty which you can use for further steps. It is a matter of the famous "intuition". Your example with the Vital Force (VF) is a good one: when the student starts with inhaling it, they first will only imagine the VF and the feeling it creates in them. After a time, the imagination will develop into a perception of truly inhaling VF. The student will be able to let go of their imagination and nonetheless be 100% sure they are inhaling VF. Then they ARE inhaling the VF. As the student knows exactly how it feels like imagining the VF they will recognize the difference, the real prickling upon their skin, the energization of their body, the Force they feel. It is more "real" than imagination.

The magician has to develop this radical self-honesty with themselves. Not only for the soul mirrors, but also for everything that follows after Step 2. Thus we have another reason to be thorough with the basic exercises: without them, the student simply lacks the abilities needed for further initiation. It is as if he would try to drive a car with closed eyes…

QUESTION 7

⊙

"AS ABOVE SO BELOW" IS SO OFTEN QUOTED IN HERMETICS I WONDER IF YOU COULD ELABORATE ON YOUR UNDERSTANDING OF THIS AND ITS SIGNIFICANCE WITHIN IIH TRAINING?

Crystalf: "Hmm, my wife told me to keep it short and simple. I'll try: Everything in hermetics is about "As Above, so below"! This is very easy to see in laboratory Alchemy. Franz Bardon's IIH represents a form of "spiritual alchemy". As above so below refers to the relationship between microcosmos and macrocosmos, in our special case the human being and the surrounding energies. I.e. the elements within the student and the elements surrounding the student. This is the reason why Bardon warns of hasting and skipping steps: condensing an element i.e. is not about playing with some random energy as some new-age philosophies implicate. It is not Reiki, some all surrounding divine energy. It is working with *yourself* in a relationship with nature itself. Thus it is like gen-technology. On the other hand, the existence of the elements is not "the Truth"™. The student constructs them by impregnating their surroundings with let's say: red colour, warmth and fire. But they can only construct in their surroundings what is already present in them. Thus if in the student "below" has a lot of anger and greed in him, the fire element they construct "above" won't be constructive and warming, but full of hate, anger and destructiveness. Neither the microcosmos nor the macrocosmos is pre-existent or has more worth than the other. In fact, the two are interdependent. And this is the case with every Element, Chakra, Sephiroth, etc.

Thus, if you want to be a blessing for your beloved, first become a blessing for yourself. If you desire the power to change reality, first learn to change your life, your attitude, your priorities. Bardon writes it in Step 8 and my own experiences go along the same lines: nothing is impossible.

Question 8

⊙

How can we know we are truly achieving the goal of a step? For example with the Vital Force, how can we know we are not fooling ourselves?

Crystalf: By working through the first exercise of Step 1 thoroughly. By observing your thoughts, you become used to observe yourself. By knowing exactly what is going on in your mind, you´ll simply be sure, if you are falling yourself or if you truly achieved something. The practice of Step 1 develops a radical self-honesty, you can use for further steps. It is a matter of the famous "intuition". Your example with the Vital Force (VF) is a good one: when the student starts with inhaling it, they first will only imagining the VF and the feeling it creates in them. After a time, the imagination will develop into a perception of truly inhaling VF. The student will be able to let go their imagination and nonetheless be 100% sure they are inhaling VF. Then they ARE inhaling the VF. As the student knows exactly how it feels like imagining the VF they will recognize the difference, the real prickling upon their skin, the energization of their body, the Force they feel. It is more "real" than imagination. Thus we are again with the theme "As above, so Below" from the last question.

The magician has to develop this radical self-honesty with themselves. Not only for the soul mirrors, but also for everything that follows after Step 2. Thus we have another reason to be thorough with the basic exercises: without them, the student simply lacks the abilities needed for further initiation. It is as if he would try to drive a car with closed eye

Question 9

⊙

Regarding the depth point in Step 5, there is a transition in the training as we touch upon new experiences. Can you tell us more about this?

Crystalf: Well, I see the depth point exercises as the central point in initiation. By reaching this stage of initiation the magician has achieved radical self-honesty, a certain control on mind, soul and body and first experiences with the nature of things outside of their own body by working with the elements. After Step 3 they could call themselves rightfully magicians. The student is "attuned" to nature. The depth point gives the magician the first access to a higher sphere of being, to his own "divine" nature. All following exercises are based on access to the depth point, the "Trance," as Bardon calls it. I don´t like the name as it implies a certain form of "half-sleeping" state. To me it is the exact opposite: To be in the depth-point means to be Awake – "I am absolutely awake, in what I am. Aware of my nature that is more than just working, eating…" The depth point leads the magician to a state where they are aware of their body, their organs, their passions, their thoughts – all at once. It is a state of BEING. That makes it magical. God defines themselves as "I am, who I am!" As BEING. Thus we first feel what it could mean to become divine and capable of creating.

Sadly, for those who at this point imagine themselves throwing fireballs, we also realize that creation, in general, is good like it is, so no need to change creation.

Question 10

⊙

As one develops a greater sensitivity within the mental, astral and physical aspects, how did you deal with and integrate these in daily life?

Crystalf: Again I have to refer to Step 1: stay focused on what you are doing at the moment. When in my mundane life I am working with clients, I am working with clients; I am not trying to deduce their biggest elementals. Bardon goes deeper into this at Step 8 – The Great NOW.

Being a magician does not mean to be a magician in a perceivable way all the time: doing clairvoyance on everybody you meet, being blatantly wise or wearing special clothes. That is a reason I don't like "Frabato" very much: it simply gives a totally wrong picture of what it means to be a magician, of the inner life of a magician. In my opinion, the book had been written from the standpoint of a quite immature student, not from someone who had no experience of its contents. If you ask me, it was meant to flatter Bardon, but the picture painted is utterly wrong. To be a magician is a state of being, of acting with self-knowledge, the flows of nature and intuition. You don't have to integrate it into your life, as it is nothing alien. It is life. The "greater sensitivity" comes as natural as learning to walk comes to a baby child. If it has to be integrated, something in your development has been left out.

Question 11

⊙

How have you managed to balance work, family and Hermetics and to integrate them?

What advice would you offer to the aspiring Bardonist?

Crystalf: Finish Step 8 before getting kids!!!!

Honestly: keep your priorities straight! To have kids is no easy decision and gives great responsibility, but great joy too. And that is true for everything we do in this life. In the second question I wrote that many people don't really want to do initiation, they want other things. In fact, they lie to themselves. This question aims in that direction. Of course: work, family, friends, hobbies, even computer games are all important and fun and take time and…and… and… but no matter what is going on: if you are sure, that you want to transform yourself into a blessing for yourself and your beloved one – thus into a magician, you'll find the time to do the exercises. On the other hand, don't forget what responsibility you have taken upon yourself. That is why I wrote: keep your priorities straight! Really be honest with yourself, what you want from life, from your situation, from your time.

Question 12

⊙

How did you make the transition between the realms and integrate them here?

Crystalf: This is all about focus. When working in magical realms, it becomes all too easy to get caught up in the transcendental side of reality. I met quite a few people who were living so much in the magical realms they seemed to nearly forget about this life here. Sadly, I think that many of these "spiritual types" even draw a lot of ego out of this behaviour. That is NOT what Bardon's books are about! Remember what he writes in Step 7 about clairvoyance: the magician must be able to turn on and turn off his clairvoyant sight at his whim and will. There is a reason why we have bodies: this is the realm where we can gain maturity. Magic is not a means to escape the problems you created in life. Quite the opposite, a magician meets up to challenges because he has realized that they are means to grow…

Question 13

⊙

Is there is anything else you would like to add?

Crystalf: Be a kind person. A looooot of people visualizing themselves as magicians in a tower, but while this is a really cool picture, these guys are mostly not the beloved ones. Look at some of the wizard types from movies and books so popular at the moment: honestly, I love towers too, but look at Saruman or Palpatine or Voldemort or other guys from the popular imagination from the last centuries: these people are not the heroes. A Bardonian magician is, in fact, a Hero. If being a magician means being a blessing to society, then a magician is a hero. So act like one! But also remember you´re human. Becoming a magician is in many ways becoming more human, and as long as you´re human you will suffer from all human weaknesses. Of course, obtaining a magical equilibrium will set you at peace with yourself, but still, other people are around and sometimes you will make mistakes while treating them. They won´t understand you, or you won´t understand them. That is life. So for me one of the main qualities a magician should have is the ability to say "Sorry!" and being sorry. It is okay not to be perfect, but to have the insight to apologize for your mistakes is crucial in the way of self-knowledge. And even when you think, you're perfectly right capable of saying sorry, when you hurt your opponent. Also, be capable of accepting an apology from another person. As you can see, I have had a lot of discussions lately about the nature of Good and Evil, and a lot of people claim, there is no such thing as good and evil, that these ideas are simply subjective. I disagree! Good people know limits in their actions, and they do not try to achieve a goal by any means. They stop when their actions inflict pain on other beings. They know compassion. Bad people only care for themselves. Don´t be a bad person. Be kind!

CHAPTER 3: DAVID PAUL COLEMAN

INTRODUCTION

David Paul Coleman is a seasoned Franz Bardon practitioner and astrologer for over twenty years. Author of *26 Keys* which is a comprehensive study guide into the workings of astrology, a great guide for hermetic practitioners since David also explains this science from a hermetic viewpoint.

David was born in 1970 in West London. He was a precocious child with a keen interest in the occult. He began reading about it at the age of six with the help and encouragement of his father. His experiences following his father's death at the age of twelve were a catalyst that started him on the path of practice and learning.

He created his first birth chart by hand in 1991 and began a twenty-year process of integrating astrology with his magical practice. Starting a small business in 1997 called 'White Dog Horoscopes' he entered the world of the internet and began connecting with others.

In the mid to late 90s he was also involved in giving talks and presentations in the UK on topics related to both magic and astrology and on a trip to Berlin he found the works of Franz Bardon and began his work with *Initiation into Hermetics*. He found that with dedication and persistence and a calm inner confidence the exercises progressed very swiftly. He found that he had a particular focus on astral magic and astral travelling, a gift that complimented his work with astrology. As a result of this his work with astrology was transformed and he changed the name of his business to 'Astral Visions.'

Since that time, Astral Visions has produced hundreds of personally written, in-depth reports on peoples astrology, more than 400,000 words, and its companion website, 'Journeys in the Astral Light' has made available a large and ever-growing collection of free material where topics are treated in-depth. David's work has also grown to include tuition and support for other initiates from many kinds of spiritual practices, given his broad knowledge of various areas, and his path led him to move to Berlin in 1999.

In the spring of 2011, David wrote *The 26 Keys*[2], which presented a new way of approaching astrology inspired by his initiation and the practice of magic described in *Initiation into Hermetic*s and the *Practice of Magical Evocation*. He was inspired to do so and lovingly assisted throughout by the beings of astrology, the spirits of the Earth Zone, the elements and the planetary spheres, and by the Spirit of Bardon. The book poured out of him in 3-4 moons and was the first draft. The cover of the book was created by his friend, Florian Forster from a design David created in 1995. It was published in the summer of 2011 and is available through Amazon.

He has made a free practice manual of the core techniques of the approach available at Journeys. Nowadays David's writing years are almost over, at least as far as Astral Visions is concerned, although he continues to post monthly articles at Journeys and is available for Skype consultations and private email discussions. His initiation is as ever-ongoing and a joy to explore, long after he completed the course of instruction in *Initiation into Hermetics*.

---

[2] https://amzn.to/3l4RyAd

Questions & Answers

Question 1

⊙

Please could you share with us a little of your IIH journey, what led you onto the path of astrology?

David: Sure. Before I was 'seasoned' (as you astrologically put it) I was lucky to have parents who not only did not oppose but actually encouraged my interest in weird things for young boys to be interested in. My father was the one to open the door first. So as a child, I was watched over and helped by him, I made myself familiar with almost every part of the occult. It was just something I was always passionately interested in. I came across a lot of stuff about astrology and magic in general, but Bardon never came up in the material. This was in the 1970s when I was about six or seven years old and living in the UK. The situation is different now, partly because of the Internet, but back then it was much more difficult to track down obscure writing, and Bardon is obscure, or at least was then.

My decision to become an astrologer started in my college years with my mother handing me a book on the subject and me drawing up my own chart and recognising it immediately as an incredibly accurate reflection of my character – it was really a huge "wow!" moment for me – and I committed fully to it in my early twenties. Shortly after that, Bardon arrived. The books were first handed to me in the German language, the original language they were written in, and like many, I immediately recognised how important they were.

The German friend who handed them to me knew I did not then understand any German, but said, "You probably already know everything in the first book, but I get the feeling that the second book has something important in it I need to pass on to you". So he did, praise him, and he was right about half of the statement, the part that came from his feelings.

Question 2

⊙

How has going through IIH shaped your life?

David: It is my life. I live it and breathe it. Therefore, it shapes everything and every moment. This was the case from the beginning.

Question 3

⊙

What were your greatest challenges following this path and how did you overcome them?

David: They are not over, they continue. Some were temporary but the most important ones are ongoing. The challenges which were overcome were helped by following the advice I was given in these books, seeking my own perception of their truth, and by not giving up.

Probably the most central challenge that is ongoing is the care and tending of the magical equilibrium. This is a task that any genuine magician devotes much of their time to and does not become complacent about. Another central challenge that is ongoing relates to the consequences that arise from an initiated awareness interacting with the world as it is today. When it is clear to the awareness that the choices humanity is making collectively are leading to a bad place, the challenge is to do something about it, or at least try to. My main concern here is with the ecosystem and the awakening of a collective healing response from us towards it, and ourselves, because the two are one.
If we are talking about astrology instead of magic, the biggest challenge was in finding a way to integrate my practice of astrology with my practice of magic. This was overcome only with time and practice. It

resulted in the material eventually being published in *The 26 Keys*. The biggest ongoing challenge as an astrologer for me is I think the biggest for all astrologers right now – discoveries about the extent of the solar system that it must assimilate. We are going to need a new paradigm for these things.

QUESTION 4

☉

WHAT HAS BEEN THE MOST REWARDING ASPECT OF THIS JOURNEY?

David: Being me and feeling happy about that. Also, the satisfaction of being able to help other people. Plus, the look on mum's face when she read the dedication in *The 26 Keys*. It will stay with me forever.

QUESTION 5

☉

PLEASE EXPLAIN TO US ABOUT ASTRAL LIGHT AND THE WORK THAT YOU DO FOR THOSE WHO DO NOT KNOW.

David: Okay, for those who know nothing at all, basically what I do is I provide a toolkit for people to explore astrology without astrologers being involved. Using this toolkit, you can gain your own personal and direct experience of your own astrology. Once you have that direct experience and understand what it can produce in your life you can start to influence it to create transformations of your circumstances and experiences. For those who know a bit about magic or who have studied Bardon, the astral light is the subtlest substance of the astral world through which astrological influences are transmitted to the corporeal world. It is the Akasha of the astral world, and the toolkit first enables you to perceive it and observe it, and then to place causations within it or to consciously transform its karma. However, one is limited to only being able to perceive and work with the astral light that relates to their being, and with the temporary current conditions represented by astrology as things move through the sky. Interacting with your astrology this way ultimately attains the same ends as the Black and White Mirrors do, because you meet with your own positive and negative qualities and are guided into working through them. It is a natural method that was used throughout the ancient world in a different format to the way I have presented it today.

Question 6

☉

For those unfamiliar with your book The 26 Keys. Could you please explain to us this work and its purpose?

David: Apart from providing you with a toolkit that I have outlined above, the main purpose of which is to provide a practical, personal experience centred, astrology for anyone with the time and interest to do so, the purpose of my book is to form a bridge between the worlds of magic and astrology and to regenerate and stimulate the discourse between them that existed in the ancient world. That's why if *The 26 Keys* is a system (I call it an approach) it is a very open-ended, 'open-source' system like IIH. It also serves to introduce the astrologer to the art of magic and the magician to the art of astrology. However, during the writing of this book, a further major purpose was communicated to me. As well as seeking to revive the ancient connection between magic and astrology, I also seek to do my part in shaping the future of astrological practice and magical practice. Both astrology and magic are at major turning points in their evolution. Astrology, in particular, is heavily challenged to remodel its paradigms to reflect modern discoveries about our solar system. Magic is ideally suited to that task. Magic, on the other hand, is at a similar turning point in terms of its coming-of-age, and astrology is well-suited to guiding it towards its future as it did in the past. These also became important purposes in my writing.

QUESTION 7

☉

PLEASE COULD SHARE WITH US THE ROLE OF THE ASCENDING PLANETARY INFLUENCES WITHIN ONE'S NATAL CHART?

David: Oh goodness that's a huge question! I will try! First, I would point out that the planets don't actually cause anything. They just resonate through their positions with what is actually happening. The basic idea is that the entire sky above us acts as a mirror for human awareness that is gazing at it (although seeing it is not required here, so the blind are also receptive, and it need not be human awareness either) and additionally it reflects what it is experiencing to that awareness in meaningful and significant ways. In modern terms, it's a very quantum idea.

That said, the structure of the solar system is taken to be a mirror for the structure of human awareness. So, everything revolves around the Sun, except for the Moon, which revolves around the Earth. Therefore, the Sun represents the core of our being (our temporary spirit or individual mental body), and the Moon takes the light of that being and reflects it as different shapes (souls, an astral awareness) towards the Earth as well as serving to transmit other things to the Earth by passing through her energetic field. She acts to shield us and all life on Earth in an immensely occulted way.

These two are the primary influences in almost every form of astrology, no matter where it is found in the world (and there are many, many different kinds of astrology). It makes sense when you realise that we observed them first. The Lights are obvious physical representations of polarity (day and night, etc.) and therefore act as conductors for the Electric and Magnetic Fluids as they interact with life on Earth.

The other planets which revolve around the Sun represent the various types of awareness that a single being experiences and has access to. Venus, for example, is basically the emotional awareness we have access to, while Mercury is the intellectual awareness we have access to. The farther we go from the Sun, the less personal and more inclusive and broad (collective) these dimensions of awareness become. This is because they take such a long time to go around the Sun that they appear to be in the same place for a long period of time and therefore do not change much from human person to person in that time.

The farther an object is away from the Sun, the more it influences things that live for longer periods of time, things which have a longer mortal lifetime, such as nations, mountains, religions or civilisations. Now consider that we just found a dwarf planet called Sedna that takes an estimated 11,400 years to orbit the Sun. She is named after the Inuit goddess of the sea and she is part of our solar system. These are not the only new arrivals by far, and there is more revelation to come. We are in a series of crises, a collective turning point.

The relationship between the various objects in the solar system is also important. As a simple example, when the Sun and the Moon face one another with the Earth between them, astrology calls it "Sun opposition Moon", which is commonly known as a Full Moon. A Full Moon is taken to have a different meaning than a New Moon (in which our Moon is between Earth and Sun). These relationships and others like them can be applied to every object in the solar system, so we can also talk about "Jupiter opposition Saturn" (Earth would be between them) when that happens, for example, these relationships astrologers call aspects.

The most significant aspects measure distances of 0, 60, 90, 120 and 180 degrees of arc between any two objects. Think of this as how the planets and the two Lights are relating to one another within us, how they get along. Signs and houses are spatial measurements used in a chart. Signs relate to where a planet is in relation to the path of the ecliptic (the apparent path of the Sun in the sky over a year), or if you prefer to its position against the stars in the sky, while houses (which I call temples) relate to where a planet is in the sky due to the rotation of the Earth (setting, rising, etc). These also influence the way an object is interpreted.

The entire system creates a complex, layer upon layer, that uniquely reflects the awareness that is being born at that moment. The significance of this fact in development and growth cannot possibly be overstated. It not only helps us to know who we are, but it also helps us to know what will make us happy, what is coming in our development and when. It shows us what things look like when we get it wrong, and supplies the remedy for those situations if that should happen.

Question 8

⊙

How can astrology assist us in IIH, in terms of aiding us going through the steps?

David: A major help is with the timing. There are certain periods every year and every month in which it is more favourable to pursue certain exercises or set yourself certain goals. It can also be hugely helpful in sorting out the Mirrors, and in transforming them. Really, the list of ways it can assist is spectacularly huge and impressive.

Question 9

⊙

You mention in your blog post that astrology has enabled you to heal yourself and others could you expand on this for us, please?

David: Sure, but I don't want to give away anybody's personal details. A lot of the help that astrology can give people seeking to heal or troubled by physical, emotional or mental difficulties is in the preventative area. Its greatest power is in shifting the astral foundations of a problem (what we feel and think that empowers it) and its magic is incredibly powerful with emotional and mental problems like depression and shyness for that reason. Physical problems take time because you must generate a strong astral and mental volt to affect a physical change but in many cases, this is also possible. It's extremely good at preventing existing problems from worsening and at minimising the possibility that serious conditions will develop.

One example I'm able to give here from recent times was how astrology helped me to identify when my own terminally ill mother was going to have a severe attack. Since I knew the 24 hour period in which this was likely to occur, I was prepared and was able to prepare others who would listen to me. In the event, she was saved from a major trauma. Healing is such a massive and broad topic that I could sit here for hours sharing similar stories with you involving astrology.

Question 10

☉

Please could you explain the relationship between the physical planets and the planetary spheres?

David: That relationship is a conceptual one. The planetary spheres are inhabited by their specific beings and entities, or Intelligences. It's where they live. The physical planets which share names with the spheres we have named (there are many others) are connected to the spheres at the mental plane level, given that they share a name. However, the physical planets do not serve to act as the physical bodies of the planetary spheres. Or at least, not for its entirety. Probably the better analogy is to think of the physical planets as a thought or a single cell of the physical body of the planetary sphere, which is spread throughout the universe and all of time and space.

Question 11

⊙

What would you say the benefits are of having IIH training behind you and studying astrology?

David: It's hard to say in general because everyone who goes through that training both starts out as and later becomes a different person, just as astrology maintains should be the case. In general, the development of the faculty of objective perception (being able to perceive the essence of things) would be an enormous benefit to chart interpretation. The magical work that the magician does with symbols would also give them a huge advantage in grasping the fundamentals of astrology (which is basically a symbolic language, more like hieroglyphs than words). If the magician is also interested in evocation, they will already be intimately familiar with many of the beings involved in our astrology.

Question 12

⊙

Through working with these planetary forces how do you guide others to overcome them?

David: Love. Often also a lot of talking about the situation looking at it from the astrological points of view. It's often immediately beneficial on a considerable scale for people to hear something like "Ah! You have Pluto on the ascendant, no wonder this is happening!" Immediately there can be a relief and a change in attitude, as it can be extremely helpful to know that there is some kind of explanation for what you are going through. And then, digging deeper, you start to work with its transformative potential, seeing it as an experience you are having as you move through your life, one that has meaning and lessons rather than just being meaningless and randomly shitty, as many people might feel. So if

I can perceive that at work, if I can see that path and its destination, I can try to find a way to help the other person see it too.

Rawn wrote in his commentary that:

> *Astrological influences affect only those things that have corporeal existence. It is geo-centric. It does not matter one within the astral or mental realms, what position a certain planet is in on the physical realm. The only effect the magician might experience in regard to ritual timing is that the physical circumstances surrounding the ritual will be eased if the astrological influences are deemed favorable, or made more difficult if they are unfavorable. This (whether positive or negative) will be seen in the preparation of the ritual space and in the ease with which any physical effect, or any effect pertaining to the astral or mental body of a corporeal entity, will be accomplished. But to the well trained magician, these effects can be easily overridden.*

And I completely agree.

Question 13

⊙

In your experience is it possible to become totally free of such influences as Bardon states in PME?

As one balances out the astral and mental aspects, such forces do not compel the magician in such a way.....

David: Being totally free of these influences means you have left the physical plane behind you, at least the Earthly physical plane. When you are physically incarnate, whether you are a vegetable or a rock, a human or a tree, if you live upon the Earth you are subject to the current resonance of the solar system. There are ways to shield yourself from various aspects of that resonance, and we always have the capacity to transform it (and thus no longer act on itself destructively), but since it always exists for us we cannot be free of it, in that case, it transforms and enlightens. We would carry it with us even if we left this planet, it's a part of the occult anatomy of everything that is born or created in and upon our world. It's like saying can we breathe without air. I am unable to recall or locate a passage in which Bardon says or even implies that total immunity to our astrology is possible.

In PME he tells us that the stars incline but do not compel (at the end of the section titled 'Magical Evocation'). This is also my view. Resonance is an astral phenomenon that is extremely receptive to influences that shape it. It is not like a dictation of what must happen. It's more like what you feel when you want to dance to something. You get to choose the moves, or not to dance at all.
Sometimes, though, the resonance for a certain thing can be extremely overpowering " –that music just always makes me cry, dammit!" – but it's temporary, and it can never negate the intention of a magician, only complicate it or make it harder.

Question 14

☉

Have you ever come across someone's natal chart that does not correspond to their personality make-up or that is contrary to it?

David: No. I have probably looked at tens of thousands of charts at this point. Every single one of them has been resonant with the personality and the life from which it must grapple and create a work of art from even someone like Bardon.

The chart is a picture of what our lives look like when we are happy, as well as being a warning about what they look like when things go awry.

Question 15

⊙

Is there anything else you would like to add?

David: Yes, thank you, a few things do come to mind here. I would like to ask everyone who reads this to spend a few minutes in contemplation of the most important planet we have.

I would also like to encourage everyone who is taking on the monumental path of initiation, no matter what method they are using to do so and to remind them to love themselves and to cherish every moment of their existence as a precious and irreplaceable thing. And then to turn that awareness upon the world around them, because we so desperately need it.

I'd like to thank my munificent patrons, the people who pay for my blog via Patreon, and the many other people who support my work physically and emotionally.

I'd also like to invite anyone who would like to contact me to do so, provided your messages are about astrology or magic. *The 26 Keys*[3] is available on Amazon in digital and paperback.

In the future, I will hopefully be offering more ways for people to learn and share with me. And I'd like to say thank you Falcon Books for giving me the opportunity to say these things.

---

[3] https://amzn.to/2VWHZcT

CHAPTER 4: JULIA GRIFFIN

INTRODUCTION

Julia Griffin is a Franz Bardon practitioner and is well known for her ability to enlighten others to find their True Self and become conscious co-creators through practical application of Universal Law. Her teachings embody advanced concepts for those who want to deepen their understanding of co-creation and personal "reality". She has a deep understanding of energetics based on extensive studies.

She is an Alchemist, Astrologer, Herbalist and Reiki Master. Julia has the ability to communicate with plants and animals. She lived with wolves for nine years, while developing her intuitive abilities.

Julia is a contributing writer for *Spirit of Maat, Drunvalo,* Melchizedek's online publication, and she also contributed to Aquarius Magazine, a publication in Atlanta, Georgia. Her notable interviews include Wayne Dyer, don Jose Luis, son of don Miguel Ruis (*The Four Agreements*), Lama Surya Das, and Robert Moss.

She has a bi-monthly radio show on 'Transformation Talk Radio' you can view on her website[4] to help in finding a higher vibration and creating a better life.

4 https://onetrueself.com/resources/articles/

Questions & Answers

Question 1

⊙

How did you come across Bardon's literature and how did it shape your life?

Julia: In 2007, a friend, who studied the angelic names, shared the practice with me. From the first, I could feel the blueprint of the angels and the uplifting of my spirit. I began memorizing the letters because I knew they were an integral point of contact with the spiritual world.

I began studying Bardon Books II and III. I loved the feeling of the colors and angels, and I was excited about having a new direction of study. I remain interested and intrigued by the depth of the study.

Question 2

⊙

Please could you tell us about some of your experiences with living with wolves?

What did you learn from these experiences including your most memorable encounter?

Julia: After my initial meeting with two wolves, I "heard" the male wolf in my mind. It was a distinctive voice, and I could feel the wolf. He was totally connected to me, and he could feel my location and physical presence. He began sharing creation myths, which were somewhat like watching a movie–marvelous in their intensity and beauty.

A couple of weeks later, I met a woman who raised wolves. Juno, her alpha female, looked deeply into my eyes, and I could feel her weighing my soul like the Goddess Maat. She found me worthy, and that feeling of acceptance flowed through me. Wolves look at the soul and heart for worthiness and value in human beings. (I could hear each wolf's individual voice after this–a portal into the animal world opened).

The wolves were quite adept. They could send messages, pictures, predict the near future, bend time, and influence the thoughts of people.

Question 3

⊙

When you communicate with plants and animals, what form does this take?

Julia: Universal light moves my consciousness into the heart space where I can hear clearly. From this point, I can ask questions, receive thoughts, and have a deeper understanding of the plant or animal. I hear words (each voice is different and individual), see images, and receive thoughts.

I feel and see the plant or animal while retaining my higher intellect. Their energy comes in waves–often with directives. (I learned how to read waves of energy from the wolves). For example, a plant may want to move to a different location, ask for nutrients, or share a secret with me. When I work with herbs, I hold the person and the formula in mind. The plants recommend leaves, colours, and roots. (Every leaf and portion on any medicinal plant is different and can amplify different qualities in a formula).

Animals tend to express their desires, give awareness of energies, which are on or off, express how they can help humans, and share recommendations for life improvements, sometimes involving colour and sounds. (Wild animals can share a tremendous amount of knowledge). Plants, animals, and nature, all want to help us with our spiritual and physical evolution.

Question 4

⊙

For those working on Step 4 of IIH, the 'Transplantation of Consciousness into animals and plants, how do you approach this and what advice would you give?

Julia: Step 4 required intention, will, time, and practice. I was intrigued by the wolves' knowledge, and I wanted to know more, which meant understanding them more and "feeling" them intensely.

While I heard the wolves almost instantly, it took practice to perceive their more complicated thoughts. It took longer with plants. I spent many hours with the wolves on a weekly basis and probably 2-4 hours daily in a garden with herbs.

Intention, purity of heart, and practice are integral to connection with the animal and plant kingdoms. I wanted understanding and knowledge of their worlds, and I wanted the joy of communication with beautiful beings such as animals and plants. When a connection is made, an incredible world is revealed.

Here are my steps:

- I ask for permission. Then, I focus on the animal or plant with universal love. A strong connection of consciousness with animals and plants is needed as well as the willingness to let go of your perception of the self. In my personal experience, I had to become more conscious of their presence (more than my own) and merge with it. I could feel the wolves and plants more than I could "feel" myself.
- I feel the sensations of the animal, plant, or person. With a plant, I might become aware of its roots, the pattern of growing leaves, the amount of moisture around the plant, and the spreading of the roots. I move INTO this feeling as part of the process.

- The feeling is followed by a complete merge, a mixing of my feelings, mind, and spirit with the plant, animal, or person. At this point, I receive information.
- There is also a trust factor. If an animal asks for a change or a relay of a message, I do it. If a plant asked for a different growing condition, I supply it. Acting on their messages usually results in a deeper connection and a more rapid transference of consciousness.
- Bardon's processes tend to provide protection with the practice. I completely agree with pulling back after making complete contact as you don't want to lose yourself or your intellect while merging with a plant, animal, or human being.

QUESTION 5

⊙

WERE THERE ANY AREAS WITHIN BARDON'S TRAINING THAT YOU FOUND WERE PARTICULARLY CHALLENGING TO YOU?

Julia: Bardon's training is intense and detailed. It is a continual study that changes and deepens as I evolve. Like the Taoist meditations, it requires a great deal of time and attention to detail as a step or process is mastered. I was pleased with the depth of connection with some of the intelligences; I was surprised at the amount of work and meditation required to fully perceive other aspects of the work.

Question 6

⊙

Do you have any tips or advice on how practitioners can gain success in VOM?

Julia: Perhaps, I am a slow learner as it took about six years to achieve this state. During this period, I intently sought the state of higher spiritual connection. At the time, my meditation practice took about 30-60 minutes on a daily basis and consisted of several small exercises. While in meditation, my wolf came and sat by me; she loved to join me for meditation. Suddenly, my mental activity ceased. It was lovely, and I felt open to universal guidance and light. Currently, it's an everyday event in my practice. For me, connection occurs consistently when in nature and when sitting in the same place on a daily basis. It's also easier to deepen the state in the first hour after awakening. When I can't connect or deepen the state, I study spiritual works, meditate more often, and take breaks to walk or rest.

Question 7

⊙

What is your opinion of Bardon's approach to astral travel? Do you feel the separation of the bodies is necessary or is an etheric double a better option for modern times?

Julia: My time with the wolves created fluidity in the astral world. They sent images and information many times each day. Sometimes, they were messages or waves of energy. They ranged from the present moment to the past and the future. I can remain in my physical body and travel as well as receiving information for myself and others. (I don't feel separation is necessary). I use a point of reference or intent for travel. I continue to work with my etheric double.

I am in the process of developing my connection but I think it is a valuable skill–and well worth the work.

Question 8

⊙

Which aspects of Bardon's training do you feel really shaped your path to where you are now?

Julia: I felt the letters and angelic names almost immediately, Waves of energy lifted my consciousness to a higher point. I worked with specific groups whenever I encountered a problem in life, and I was surprised at how I quickly experienced new and positive feelings in place of lower ones.

When I intensified my study by studying the elements and letters, life flowed in a more harmonious way. New solutions came into my life, and I felt hopeful and more open to life.

Over time, the work changed my perceptions about myself and life. It helped in overcoming karmic patterns and led to a field of greater possibilities. I felt supported by the energetics of the practice.

I gained hope and insight from my experience with the letters and names of the heavenly host. Once mastered, it is a way of moving into a higher state of being, encountering higher frequencies, and using inherent spiritual gifts.

Question 9

⊙

How did your reality and working through this in terms of lifestyle change and shape your reality?

Julia: Metaphysics states emotions are the test of mastery. As a natural intuitive, I was very emotional and felt the "waves" of situational challenges as well as the emotions of others.

Through the study of Bardon's work including the angelic names and letters, I found that I could detach and move into a higher state through the use of these two tools. When emotions are turbulent, it's difficult to find a higher frequency, which is a source of knowing and true answers. The alteration in my emotions led to additional time for study, meditation, and listening to my inner self. This shift led to an alteration of my physical habits and my understanding of energy, which enhanced my gifts.

Question 10

⊙

Regarding your forthcoming title "A Modern Guide to the Cosmic Letters," I wonder if you could tell us more about this title and how it can aid people in everyday life?

Julia: *A Modern Guide to Cosmic Letters,* presents slightly different methods of tapping into the energies and virtues of the letters. It serves as a quick guide for learning the letters, but it also lists detailed information in the appendix. The Guide is composed of my notes and insights, which came into being through the process of learning and delving into the meaning and frequencies of the letters. By teaching basic information about the letters, I refined much of the information.

Initially, I studied the letters to heighten my ability with the angelic names. Over time, a colour or letter would appear in answer to a question or a desire to solve a problem. The letters appeared in my mind with exquisite, shining colour, and I could feel the qualities of the letter. As my work deepened, I found that the letters (alone) could create a great deal of positive change. I teach the letters in this format to my students, who had similar experiences. The letters, their colors, and virtues would simply come to them, providing aid on an energetic level.

Question 11

⊙

How do you use the Cosmic Letters when working with your clients?

Julia: I use the colour of a letter. I experience the colour, then send the colour to the client while describing it and its effect on consciousness. (I don't identify it as a letter.) I ask them to visualize the colour often and to imagine the desired shift of consciousness. When possible, I transmit the colour to them by seeing the letter and its colour and feeling the energy in my field with the correct elemental placement, radiating it to the person, and erasing the letter after reception. Sometimes, I create journeys with the energy of the letters. For example, I may use the image of a cave with dark opal walls, a blue-green pool with emerald green moss around it, and a mermaid with a blue-green tail. The imagery helps with feeling love in the physical world, creating abundance, and feeling positive emotion. (J=dark opal), (M=blue-green), (G=emerald green) I also have an exercise, "The Colors of Water", which we often use in class to quiet and clear emotions. We study the angelic names in some of my classes. More advanced students and clients study the names in greater depth. TARATO, Cancer 10, Angels of Weather, and YLEMIS, Pisces 29, Angels of Divine Love, are favourites.

Question 12

⊙

With all of the current chaos in the world, how have you used the Cosmic Letters to maintain your equilibrium during this time?

Julia: Many intuitive's experience a heightened awareness of the collective energies surrounding them. It's accurate to allude to the presence of fear and hate with the current epidemic and racial riots. The collective energy is often agitated.

Working with the letters during this time brings clarity and peace—and separation from the lower collective energies. Meditation on the letters raises my consciousness to a higher point. I remember the value of feeling peace and connection with the higher self and the importance of radiating it throughout my field and in the space around me.

The Cosmic Alphabet reconnects my consciousness to Source so that I receive inspiration, intuitive messages, and alignment. It gave alignment with the spiritual feeling of connection–the marvelous feeling when the universe moves you through life and its ensuing sensation of clarity and knowing.

Chapter 5: Justin B the Magician

Introduction

Justin B is a dedicated practitioner of magic and artist. Justin began his journey at the age of eighteen. He is an explorer and adventurer whose curiosity for life and adventure lead him on a journey into of magic. Having over twenty years of practice and worked his way through Bardon's three books and now has been given his own system of Kabbalah. He continues to research and explore the infinite universe that surrounds us.

Justin has a blog named 'Perennial Magic'[5] which you can follow.

[5] https://justinbthemagician.wordpress.com/

Questions & Answers

Question 1

⊙

Please could you share with us how you began on the path of magic?

Justin: From many unusual and odd experiences from a very young age such as sleep paralysis as well as seeing a "goblin" wide awake during the day, I knew the world was not how most people believed it to be. When I was around fourteen or so I had an intense release of Kundalini energy which from the fear of the experience created something of a demonic tulpa. This being could perform a certain poltergeist-like activity and would try to possess me. Luckily for me, a fellow student at school who was very gifted helped me remove this entity and I began my journey at the age of eighteen practising Qi Kung and energy work as shown to me from that same friend who was very gifted at psychic perception. He had a very unique method of teaching where it just seemed so simple and direct. Rather than arduous training and practice, it was more about getting better at focus and perception.

I then picked up some books on something called "the empty force" that I practised for several years. The description was simple but in practice, it can be arduous. Its main practice was holding a horse stance and keeping an empty mind for an hour. You had to do this every day for three years. Needless to say, this helped a great deal when I started Bardon's thought control exercise. Later, I began to dabble with ceremonial magick and spirit work, doing the LBRP and the watchtower rituals. This led me to work deeply with the four archangels of the quarters as spirits I would evoke daily. Some of the ideas they shared with me which I shared with a friend who was a Yogi/Bardon magician led him to give me his copy of IIH because he said they were aligned, and they were. So, I started IIH at the age of twenty-three.

It must have been great to have found Bardon's IIH so early on?

Justin: Didn't seem so at the time. That was why I went with Bardon. It was difficult to get past the symbols and inspirations from spirits with my internal chatter or expectation of what they may say, even from years of meditation. You see, this is before the internet had taken off. If you did not know someone who could advise you it had to be worked out on your own, no validation unless it worked. So when I would work with spirits or the archangels I kept questioning if it was some internal garbage within me or pure inspiration from a spirit. Bardon was a great guide in ways in which I needed to focus and clear the mind. That is also why I recommend Neo-Reichian exercises of tension and relief and Wim Hof. It really helps clear the thoughts.

Question 2

⊙

Interestingly you speak about 'tension' in the body, Please could you expand on this a little more?

Justin: First you must realize that most of your internal chatter, emotional colouring of experiences and reactions to things is due to internalized, repressed speech or expression. Think about small children. If left to their own devices they are chatterboxes. They give direct commentary about everything they experience, and their imaginations are free to run wild and their emotions flow out. Parents or adults then impress the social norms, and teach them to suppress their unending dialogue from being voiced. It does not go away though.

The speech, the imagination and all the rest is still pumping away. Watch an adult think about what they are about to say and if you watch closely you will see muscle tension around the throat and jaw. That builds over time, as do emotional responses we must "cover up" because they are not accepted. What the psychotherapist attempts is to relive the experience that created it, which does not help or helps very little only when the patient experiences a release of the tension (why confession feels so good and freeing) what really needs to take place is a full release of body tension.

You experience this at times when you have had a long hard day of work, or physical strain. After such massive strain you flop down and feel as you could melt, your mind is at peace and you drift off into rest. That feeling of peace, of release, is really just that! Having a temporary release of the tensions in the body brings that bliss and inner silence which is why hard work has always been so lauded in society; it gets things done and has the added benefit of energetic release.

Meditation is another way to do this by essentially starving the stimulus of the senses which allows the inner experience to pour out. If we first work with the muscles tension in the body before we do meditation we will see a profound difference in reaching higher states of consciousness and focus. There is no tension holding you within the confines of the body and you are allowed to surf the waves of blissful awareness even if a part of your body feels pain.

The simplest way, but not the most thorough, is to take a deep breath, hold it while you strain every muscle in a certain muscle group and release the muscles in that group and the breath when you have reached the limit of your ability to hold it. Start with the feet and move up to the head. Scan the body to find any sources of tension and repeat the exercise in that area while being fully open and aware of the area. You will see a marked difference in your ability to meditate. Jack Willis wrote a fantastic free book that is available online that covers many exercises to fully release the tension and the proper breath to do this with. Wim Hof breathing and physical stretching is another amazing way to do it.

QUESTION 3

⊙

RELEASING TENSION IN THE BODY AND FOCUSED AWARENESS. HOW ARE THEY RELATED?

Justin: That is a great segue in this discussion because one moves into another. Once you release body tension you will notice more and more the field of awareness grows, you get a sense of what your energy feels like and how to move it. The old trick of thinking about your small toe on your left foot is a good example. Prior to being directed to experience that little digit, it was most likely out of your awareness, but once directed your awareness flashed down to it. Grade that awareness though, was it a gentle vague cloud of perception or was it deep and penetrating such as when you stub that toe in the dark and you feel every heartbeat within it and the nerves flash like a bolt of lightning. Expanding, strengthening and purifying the state of awareness leads (just as tension and relaxations led to awareness) to psychic states of awareness.

The more you work on your awareness the more in the moment and perceptive it is, the more you are open to direct experience in a deeper way from your senses. Your psychic senses are just your normal senses in a more perceptive state. With experience and observing the cycles and patterns in nature, the higher realms become as obvious as the nose on your face, always there but slightly out of awareness.

Question 4

⊙

Within studying magic there can be a difficulty in the discernment between imagination and genuine experience when dealing with the subtle realms. How do we avoid the trap of fantasy?

Justin: That is an excellent point. Imagination that is not charged with 'will energy' is fantasy. It takes training to work both skills to do magic. Working one gives you great mental vistas and vision, the other the ability to succeed. When united they can do wonders. Now, having said that a purified and trained imagination is better than a mirror to scry in (the mirror is only a physical symbol of the imagination, an object on which the conscious mind and soul have agreed they can communicate).

Observe the imagination and become aware of its actions, its movements, its creations. This is what magic orders really do from ancient times until now. You receive a set of symbols that represent actual subtle forces in the universe. One learns through awareness and meditation what that force is like and links the experience of the energy signature to the symbol the order has prescribed. Through training and ritual, this works just as well as me saying the word "cow" and a picture of a cow appears in your mind imaginatively without your will being involved. The imagination so trained can be gazed into and the products that appear will show you exactly what forces are at work around you better than any astrological chart could. Here is where the magic comes in, one then either charges the forces at work to increase their power around you or one can banish it, or add a symbol charged with the will force so it interacts with the other forces on your behalf. There, the whole of practical magic laid bare. It is so simple no one believes it or uses it until shown repeatedly that it works. To get back to the point on fantasy though that has always been the warning of the astral plane, it is filled with illusions and deceptions. Yes, because the imagination has not been purified and properly trained to see and interpret the language being discussed. It is like reading a story in another language you either barely understand versus it being read by a master of literature in that language.

Where magic differs from literature thankfully is the reader once trained can interject their own story upon it.

QUESTION 5

☉

FOR THOSE WORKING ON STEP 3. IF SOMEONE IS WORKING ON DEVELOPING THE ANALOGOUS ELEMENTS HOW DO THEY KNOW IF THEY ARE REALLY TAPPING INTO IT? OR JUST THEIR IMAGINATION?

Justin: I think the best way to describe this and Bardon even mentions this in regards to evocation and people don't really hone in on that concept much. Go out into a graveyard at night with no light, or go deep inside a cave in pitch black or into a dank dark cellar. Now call to an evil spirit. Or if that is too scary go into a dark room and convince yourself someone is behind you and about to get you. If you are imaginative and spiritually inclined you probably already have goosebumps, shaking your head "no way!" If you get the point you don't actually need to do the above, you understand the power of the imagination already. You see we assign power to the imagination in one area but when we say conjure the fire element around you it seems an impossible feat. When you can imagine at will an element, in the same way, fear can force you to imagine a boogeyman, then you have attained a certain level of power both in quality and in quantity. I have done some experiments with students who could not magically tell the difference between a gnome or an angel from Geburah on whether or not they could influence one psychically another simply by observing some pictures before doing a group meditation.

I found that if two people in a group of 6 observed several pictures of a certain artistic quality and the other four were simply directed to observe their imagination, that the imagery would be similar in quality to the images seen by the other two. So, if you are having troubles with an element or force find some form of an artistic medium that would help you fill the imagination with the ideas associated with the force, just like people watch horror movies on Halloween. You may not think it is psychically or magically effective but it does have an influence on the mental and astral forces around you. Feed your head properly. Another point I would like to discuss here is as you develop your skills you may have peak moments and plateaus of experience. The peaks are when you break through to a better quality or quantity of force, where the plateaus are your normal or average levels. When working around others though who have not raised their levels to what you have attained then they experience a difference. If one meditates on this they will see this is why a magician can affect healing on another but may find it difficult to heal themselves.

Also, don't "demand" the way another experiences an element or force. I once did a teaching session at a local meditation centre years ago. I was discussing the elements and I was teaching how one can better work with the elements through vibrating the names of the quarter angels and meditating on their qualities. I simply demonstrated the proper way to vibrate the name, Raphael. After I had several people come to me and say that they all had experiences related to the air element. One described a certain smell (one I associate with air that they had no experience with), some described feeling a breeze and one heard wind chimes. The element affected them each in their own way. Don't demand an experience be the way you desire, just draw it and allow it to work.

So many magicians are too focused on control which diminishes their power actually. How much will does it take for me to conjure the idea of a book in your mind? If you were sensitive as you read the word, maybe you saw a perfect representation of a book in your visual field, maybe you recalled the smell of old yellowing pages or freshly printed paper? Perhaps you heard a book shut tightly. Either way, your imagination with a simple prompt came alive, it may have even caused a flash of will which will cause you to go find the book that appeared to you in some way, whichever was best for you. What power awaits to be aroused in you simply by allowing it to come forth!

Question 6

⊙

What are your experiences with going through IIH, did you find it was sufficient or did you find it necessary to search out supporting literature?

Justin: To really explain my view of Bardon it is of course necessary to look at the time and place of his writing, of the magical writings of the time, and what he was trying to accomplish. I sometimes ask myself if Bardon wrote IIH today would he have written every word of it like he did then? I honestly think not. The core or essence is the same of course, but if you have ever written instructions for another you know how difficult that can be, especially if you can have no interaction or dialogue with that person during or after the reading.

I recommend writing instructions on even a simple mundane task as if the reader has no prior knowledge of the subject. It is quite enlightening. So, that is how I look at all magical instruction books. The author has a set of experiences and wishes to convey them in a meaningful way to the reader, but because the subject is the subtle forces of magic it makes it even more difficult. How do you teach it?

That is why I always recommend a few other systems be read at least. Get a few maps for the territory. IIH for me specifically, I always compare to a technical manual on building a complex machine like a car.

Remember at the time of Bardon writing IIH the only way you could learn occultism is if you joined a magical order, swore oaths, and were trained in a certain set of symbols to be used. Bardon was one of the few who tried to keep his oaths and was trying to go to the public with the work. It was not until later that magical orders started having their secrets fall into public consumption. So, if you took all of the work of the Golden Dawn and kept your oaths of secrecy but tried to publish an instruction manual on the path to spiritual enlightenment and magical development you would have to teach someone to build their own personal magical order.

So, going to a magical order for training is like buying a car at a dealership where Bardon is teaching you how to build a car from scratch. I always try to impress this concept on those coming to me with questions on Bardon. The secrets are all out there, we are flooded in them so they seem of no value. Bardon did not have this world, it was all hidden away. What would he write now with the secrets of so many orders available online?

I did not see this point right off though, I went through the work and realized it as I went. So, for me having worked using Bardon's methods, I like to see it as having given me an insight into any magical system or order. It is a *Tabula Rasa* for magic in my mind. An almost scientific journal from which one can penetrate the meaning of any system or symbolism, even for instance, Enochian magic or Thelema. I think a good study of IIH with that perspective would benefit any magician no matter their belief system or practice.

Question 7

⊙

Which aspects did you find the most challenging going through Bardon's books?

Justin: The soul mirror, which I think is everyone's biggest challenge. It was not until I took a Jungian Active Imagination approach that I really had great success with it. I tried it all, from will work, sigils, autosuggestion, the magic of food and drink EmoFree and I must say, that the book *The Inner Guide Meditation* by Edwin Steinbrecher is an excellent resource (I found it much later sadly) but If I had to do it again I would focus on a Neo-Reichian approach first with some Jungian Active Imagination for balance which is what the Steinbrecher book is all about with Astrology added.

Honestly, I am not a fan of the methods Bardon chose to work on balancing the soul mirror, I think if he had more modern methods he would have chosen those. I think an honest, unflinching look at one's soul is needed and valuable but creating lists of hundreds of issues will not fix anything. It is discovering the need within the issue. Every negative trait or quality arises from a behaviour that was acquired to defend and protect the ego. Only by facing the need and releasing the tension can healing begin and balance achieved. The positive trait will then bloom on its own from the released psychic or emotional tension. A good astrological chart can be of great assistance in discovering hidden problems.

Question 8

⊙

Which step took you the longest and why?

Justin: If I look at my work from a strictly IIH perspective Step 8. Not because of the difficulty but because that is where I did the most magical experimentation. If IIH was a college I probably majored in the evocational arts. This of course translated later into kabballah. I delved deeply into their study for several years with a good portion of my blog devoted to that part of my work.

Question 9

⊙

How would you describe the difference between astral projection and mental projection?

Justin: I think most methods online focus on mental projection which can gently lead to astral projection with practice. I had sleep paralysis as a child so anything coming close to astral projection instantly caused panic. For me, mental projection which eventually allowed me the freedom and peace to allow myself to astrally project was the way to go. Let me just say this: when you astrally project there is no doubt you have done so. It is not a very vivid mental projection or guided imagery, it is an experience that changes you. You still have a slight perception at first that a residue of your awareness and personality is within your flesh but 99% of your consciousness is out and that is when you KNOW beyond doubt another world exists (that is if the Other has not found you prior to this as it did me). The difference is night and day. Like Gordon White says it is like "becoming invincible".

QUESTION 10

⊙

IN STEP 5 THE DEPTH POINT EXPLAINED IN RAWN'S COMMENTARY WE LEARN ABOUT THE INFINITELY FINITE POINT

CAN YOU SHARE ANYTHING MORE ABOUT THE SIGNIFICANCE OF THIS PART OF THE JOURNEY AND HOW THIS LINKS ON TO SUBJECTS SUCH AS THE PERSONAL AND UNIVERSAL AKASHA?

Justin: Be open, be empty. If you look at IIH, and this is some of the genius of what Bardon did, you see the training builds on itself. Learning vacancy is a warm-up lesson to working with the depth point and akasha. So, when students of IIH have not yet done the vacancy work and ask questions about the depth point it is a struggle because even the relatively simple experience of vacancy has not been perceived (not to say anything of the deeper and more profound experiences that one can achieve through vacancy). It is like not having learned your numbers in elementary school but asking how division works.

I can give an answer but it will do you little good. With that being said read up on what Peter Carroll says on the force of Chaos, also what Steiner said on the Akasha or Chaos and how it works. Go out into the country and find a large flat piece of land. Layout under the stars. See in the constellations how even the gods play through their cycles in the night sky. Think of space and everything contained within it. Know that you are made up of mostly empty space with charged particles in a somewhat distinct order that is completely changed out every so often, yet you appear on initial inspection to be "the same". You too are a constellation in a way. Seek the part of you that all life comes from, all feelings and thoughts. Where is the root of your consciousness, its depths? Every river has its source, you are a river of experience. The source is your depth point.

QUESTION 11

⊙

ONCE COMPLETING IIH HOW DID THE QUALITY OF YOUR COMMUNICATION WITH SPIRITS CHANGE?

Justin: In a classic full-circle story I realized what initially brought me to Bardon, the fact that I could not finely slice whether a spirit's "words" were coming from the spirit, or were my creation or if they met somewhere in between was finally achieved. I knew after so much work with the spirits that they have no "language" other than energy, as in they are energy and their interaction with us produces certain cognitive experiences. The more similar we are in our views, culture and life experience the more similar our experiences with the spirit will be.

If I sat down and did an evocation with someone from a radically different culture we would have some perception differences but the overall message would be the same. I have tried these experiments and they work. That is what a tribal group, coven or order has by being together, a shared language and symbol set from which the spirit or god is experienced for easier communication. So, once I learned that really the important thing is the awareness and experience of the spirit or god's energy, then some of my big questions started to get answered. Yes, I could translate the shared energy into a dialogue for many people to understand but to me, it was energy moving and flowing between two conscious beings. The practice is like quietly being engaged in music that makes you feel something. Vacancy of mind and single-pointed focus are paramount in this. Let me also say, you can clothe these forces in denser energies. I have seen some wild things. It is novel and can be a confirmation but it is eventually pointless and a real hassle to get accomplished.

Question 12

⊙

You have shared some very detailed correspondences with various beings. In your writings. Have you noticed a difference between 'Bardon' spirits and other spirits?

Justin: For me, Bardon's catalogue of spirits are an odd breed. Energetically they are very different than say calling Ophiel or Uriel. They are very inclined to teach and yet they are reserved. If you go in with intentions they don't find proper I have seen some of them straight up ignore a magician or give them a brush off answer. Very funny sometimes, actually! Once had some dilettantes wish to evoke a Bardon spirit so I explained how it could be done, they tried it and they told me the spirit requested they plant a tree and it would help them with the task. They did so but the task was not completed. I just saw it as the spirit teaching them a lesson.

Just from my experience, Bardon spirits are more selective in what they do or whom they work with. Also, appearance-wise they somehow "look" different. Maybe more modern is the word. I will let the intrepid student discover more, and maybe that is just how they act towards me or those I have spoken with. I have had a few other Bardon magicians tell me the same but again they lived in my cultural and temporal location. The exception to that seems to be the elementals. They appear to be more willing to work with even non-Bardon magicians in similar ways other spirits do. There is only one spirit from Bardon's PME I still dialogue with and that is only when a nice thunderstorm rolls in.

Question 13

⊙

HOW DID YOU BEGIN TO DEVELOP YOUR CONNECTION TO YOUR HGA? AND ONCE ESTABLISHED HOW DID YOUR LIFE CHANGE?

Justin: I have seen many descriptions and explanations on the HGA. I started with Bardon's automatic methods for communication which gave me a "name" which I later found out had meaning in Yiddish which I thought was fun.

The most dramatic and life-changing work came the first time I did the (little did I know at the time that it was mistranslated) Bornless ritual. I began using it before evocations and no matter what spirit I called I first got this powerful presence.

When I dug deeper into the Bornless and discovered its history and how it is actually, 'The Headless Rite', I used it in much the same manner Crowley recommends in *Liber Samekh.* I did daily invocations and spent as much time focusing my mind on the force. After several years of this, I recommend the practice.

I have seen many descriptions and explanations on the HGA. I started with Bardon's automatic methods for communication which gave me a "name" which I later found out had meaning in Yiddish which I thought was fun. The most dramatic and life-changing work came the first time I did the (little did I know at the time that it was mistranslated) Bornless ritual. I began using it before evocations and no matter what spirit I called I first got this powerful presence. When I dug deeper into the Bornless and discovered its history and how it is actually 'The Headless Rite,' I used it in much the same manner Crowley recommends in *Liber Samekh.* I did daily invocations and spent as much time focusing my mind on the force. After several years of this, I recommend the practice.

For me, the real key is just opening yourself up and giving yourself to the highest, make the connection to it and allow it to guide you and to work on you. It can be as simple as a single-pointed focus and focusing on your highest state of mind or consciousness. Open yourself to that force and know that everything that you see, hear, read, occurs is a message from the highest working on you for your development. BOOM, the practice will skyrocket if you can do that. Don't think of some baby with wings but you can if that helps. Also, the message may be an hour or days after.

The real key is truly focusing on the divine connection within your consciousness and being open to inspiration for a time. As my best friend and fellow magician used to half-joke it is just "You from the future". Think of yourself at your most divine, your most inspired, your most compassionate, your most insightful, conscious and potent. That is it. Allow that energy to work on and reside in you now. Once you can connect to that, magic is actually as simple as inner dialogue or like pillow talk with a divine lover. Let go of your desires, open yourself to the divine by creating a space for the divine to manifest and work in and through you. It is the merger of prayer and magic. As the medicine man Fools Crow said, "Become a hollow bone."

Question 14

⊙

Where do you see your magical path leading?

Justin: In the past few years I have finally answered a lot of the remaining questions I had. It was a long arduous process and in many ways it was for me like going into the lab every day and doing research on the structure and nature of the universe. I had a lot of questions I wanted answers for, and which I did not want; or in my younger days, did not have someone to just give them to me. I had a couple of guides but they were human.

My major drive in magic, evocation and similar works was the drive to just find the truth. Another person can give you only their perspective, not the truth as you can experience it. The finger pointing at the Moon. So, once I had the answers I sought I had a period of time where I felt sort of lost.

What do I do now?

The answer was of course what step 10 in Bardon is about. You develop your perception, your ability, your consciousness to divine levels. You manifest spirit into matter, the work of the Sun described in the Emerald Tablet. This also translates for me in my work with others and my art. I am beginning to work on some things and have been doing experiments with art and paintings as a way to help others work with magical forces. Probably in the next year or two I will do commissioned paintings as talismans of sorts for people who would like a certain magical force in their lives or just a piece of magical art.

I would recommend the following:

1. Keep a journal of weird experiences, synchronicities, magical results, recurring or odd dreams, and things that seem magical that occurred to you. Go back and read it every now and then. There is something in our consciousness that likes order and structure, that tries to pull the veil over our eyes. Magic plays with that order and structure, it pulls the veil open. So anything too unusual will be pushed away or forgotten by the conscious mind. Remind yourself now and again the world is weird. Realize you will probably never cast physical fireballs to amaze your friends and even if you could somehow do it, doing so would disrupt the observer's psyche so much it would be fairly close to rape in terms of disturbance. Because of that same mechanism that protects your conscious mind from the weird it also protects others from the weird. They would most likely suppress the experience and develop some odd behaviour to compensate for the tension caused. Usually, magic works in giving you an advantage, by increasing your odds and making something more likely to occur. However, if you get some fairly weird magicians together by themselves you will get some weird alterations in reality. A magician; once they realize where real power comes from, becomes a gateway for the divine to work miracles.

2. Adopt Chaos magic's philosophy of "Use what works" if it does not work try something else. Find what works. This is not a free pass to jump from system to system, you have to put in the work, but if chanting a classic mantra for the element of fire does not help aid the imagination or inspire you try something else that does, even if it is imagining throwing a fireball.

3. .Most importantly, there is no race for magical development going on. Savour the work. Enjoy the experience. See every challenge as a gift from the divine to develop yourself. This is yours, all yours. Take your own time as you need. Be honest with yourself. Don't see this life or this world as something to escape from, but see it as your mission to use the gifts given to you and the skills you have acquired to make this world more divine. That is why we are truly here. The philosophers stone is really our own transformed soul, use it to make the world around you golden. Ask yourself. is your work your own or someone else's? You can talk shop with other magicians, be inspired, moved or guided but your path should always be your own. Be who you are. Share your light. Be a force of nature.

Question 15

☉

Is there anything else that you would like to add or feel should be covered?

Justin:

- Always keep in mind this simple fact, when magic seems too difficult or complex: Cave men figured it out on accident.
- Study shamanism, its views and beliefs and try to extract the workings behind what they did versus ceremonial magic or Bardon magic. They have distinct things in common.
- Grab hold of those similarities and realize the rest is just trying to get everyone on the same page linguistically on what to do with these forces that occur naturally.
- Ponder for a bit what is the difference between a shaman, a psychic, a witch or a magician or someone who is extraordinarily lucky, or a genius, or someone possessed of mind-blowing talent?
- Are they using the same force in different ways?
- How could all of these groups get similar results with drastically different belief structures and means?
- I have seen someone with no training or magical experience who was so afraid of magic read a spell that produced stronger results than a ceremonial magician with years of experience trudging through an incantation. What did one tap into that the other could not?

Chapter 6: Martin Faulks

Introduction

Born in 1977 in England, Martin Faulks is known internationally as a meditation master, adventurer, spiritual warrior and author. Martin's years of discipline and dedication to daily meditation practice have led to mundane and spiritual achievements. His demonstrations of mind over matter using the power of meditation brought international attention which was documented in the press. Such skills include: altering his body temperature, changing the binary waves in brain function, and retention of breath underwater. These demonstrations have highlighted the potential of ancient mind sciences for healing, health, spirituality and self-development. These demonstrations are available on his successful YouTube Channel under the name of, *The Power of Meditation*.[6]

Known as the *mnemonic magus* Martin is thought to be the first person since the renaissance to master the magical memory methods of Giordano Bruno.

Martin also runs the Seshen Hermetic Meditation School,[7] which focuses on progression through the universal path taught by Franz Bardon. You can also follow him on his website.[8]

---

6 https://www.youtube.com/playlist?list=PL118EEB543A4F43FE

7 https://www.facebook.com/SeshenHermeticMeditation

8 https://martinfaulks.co.uk/

Questions & Answers

Pleroma

by Martin Faulks (July 2016)

When I was young I felt drawn to meditation. Every day I used to sit and practice the ideal state of mind. Then I would try to bring that awareness, goodwill and inner tranquillity into my daily life.
Later on,
I found myself drawn to meditate in different places,
In the noise of the city,
In the calm of the woods,
Next to the sea,
Or in sacred spots.

As time passed I found myself practising my art in places which made it harder to keep a calm focus. I found myself searching places and situations of adversity and distraction.

But as my ability deepened another change occurred,
I became transported in my mind's eye,
As if I was entering a realm of pure consciousness
Or going into some dream.
With daily practice, I found I could rise
Through various areas of this world,
Each more beautiful and subtle than the next.
Through star-like realms
And areas of pure beautiful light I rose.

Whenever I found myself unable to go further
I sat patiently in calmness
And found with daily persistence,
My heart was purified,
And I would ascend higher.
Now I sit at the gates of the place we go to when we finally wake up and our body is no more.

Perhaps one day the doors will open and I can sit in gentle contemplation within.

Question 1

⊙

Please could you share a little more of your journey with us, from growing up with this ideal to manifesting it?

Martin: Thank you very much for including my poem in the interview. Creative writing and allegorical tales have always been an important part of human nature, a way of expressing ideas and concepts, in a way that is easy to understand and approachable.

Growing up stories were very important to me. As a child, I had no concept of a Hermetic Adept or Bodhisattva, but I felt a calling and searched my environment to find something which it matched to. I found myself fascinated by mythological tales and heroic figures. For me the idea that some special event, discovery or process could suddenly reveal our inner potential, or bestow us with special abilities, was fascinating.

I spent a lot of time reading comics and watching films and always felt that the radioactive spider, magic potion, or special discovery was just around the corner. As time progressed and I grew older, I started to look at practical ways to improve myself and to move towards the goal. I dedicated my time to the practice of martial arts and spent as much of my waking life practicing as possible. My best friend and I attended three martial art classes a day, five days a week. We truly believed in our teacher and the art we were practising. So much so, we often took things at face value even when they didn't work.

I remember when we were given a book that claimed to have methods of performing a special form of meditation that would lead to us gaining the power of seven men. We sat in the positions it described and followed the breathing exercises exactly. We were very disappointed when we didn't see any significant change in our physical strength. Likewise, when we were taught pressure points that were supposed to immobilise or knock an opponent unconscious, we were disappointed when practising with one another that they didn't seem to do anything other than cause pain, no matter how hard we hit. Our instructor informed us that they were very, very specific points and had to be hit very accurately. So we paid an acupuncturist to mark on our bodies the exact locations and struck them with a hammer, only to find that once again they were ineffective.

As we progressed through our teenage years our explorations went further afield and we discovered Buddhism and yoga, a discipline my friend dedicated his whole life to. I was searching for something more, to me, the yogic texts were not open about the purpose of their exercises and I felt that many of the practices were confused and incomplete. I researched into the Western traditions and found ritual magic, but to me, the long drawn out words and readings, the figures drawn up in the air and memorised routines were a barrier to interacting with these spiritual forces, not an aid. I wanted to go directly to the source in order to control, see and interact with the magical force itself.

I started designing my own system based on the elements. I sat in contemplation as to how to directly contact and make a connection with the hidden forces. I called this path 'Elementalism' and truly felt I was creating something new. About that time, as fate often does, a gift appeared in the form of a book called *Modern Magic* by Donald Michael Craig. Amongst the exercises, some rang true for exactly what I was attempting to do. I asked at Atlantis Books (a shop in London) about the sources and this is when I discovered *Initiation into Hermetics*. The moment I opened up the book I knew it was something special. The very system I was attempting to recreate from some distant memory lead it to my hands.

I was just sixteen years old and it took me a year to establish a solid routine, starting and stopping and often becoming discouraged, but after my seventeenth birthday, I managed to remain stable. Since then, I have practised for two hours every day, missing only one session in the years that followed. At the age of thirty-nine, I can honestly say this has been the most rewarding practice of my life, something that I view as the greatest blessing and the most wonderful honour.

Question 2

⊙

When you spoke about creating an 'ideal state of mind' in this discourse. What methods did you use to aid you in developing and maintaining this?

Martin: I have always practised the magical training regime outlined in Franz Bardon's system and I believe this to be the most effective, balanced and safe regime of Hermetic training available. Whenever I have found it hard to make progress, to master an exercise or to develop an ability, I have looked around the world and searched for someone or a tradition who have specialised in that area. I would find a way to spend time learning from them, training and just being around people who are better at what I am trying to do.

To begin with, my training was all about mastery of the exercises laid out within Bardon's books. My focus was on developing these abilities and improving my mastery of the spiritual powers. Little did I know, by neglecting everyday matters in favour of a complete emotional and intellectual focus on the Hermetic path, I was missing out on one of the most important aspects. In truth, our training is to change our everyday waking consciousness. This is an insight that not many when they first start the path, are ready or able to see. As I travelled from teacher to teacher and from tradition to tradition, I started to gain more of an insight into this mystery. And in this sense, the most sublime teachings can be found in the most mundane.

Through our spiritual exercises, we improve all of our mental faculties – our memory, our imagination, the clarity of thought, emotional integration and balance, awareness, the ability to stay on target, our concentration, our goodwill, compassion and virtue. All of this training creates ripples which transfer into daily life. However, if you make your exercises your focus of your daily existence, you can actually sometimes forget to fully employ and transfer the abilities you have gained through your training into every waking moment. For this reason, it is important to make life the focus, not the exercises.

In a sense we need to live a magical life, to use our spiritual abilities in every moment. This I believe is one of the most powerful methods of training, to make sure that Hermetic skills are a part of your everyday skill set. So when you talk to others, you practise your clairvoyance, by sensing the energies surrounding the situation, emotions and true goals the person has inside of them. When washing, you rid yourself of negativity. When you dress, each item of clothing has significance and power. When you lock your front door, you send a wave of protection around your house. When you kiss a loved one goodnight, you pass a blessing to them. You put your intention in your letters and emails. You send a healing force to those you meet who are ill. In this way, you use the abilities you have gained through your Hermetic training in every waking moment. This has turned out to be the most powerful lesson in training for me.

Question 3

⊙

Could you please explain the turning point in your life where you felt a shift in consciousness and a coming out of duality into oneness.?

Martin: The Hermetic path is truly beautiful, in that it is ongoing and unfolds in many subtle and interconnected ways. Sometimes you will find that your progress comes with big breakthroughs or epiphanies that dramatically change your perception of the world. Often it is a gradual and an almost imperceivable process in which your understanding, and indeed your capacity for understanding, are growing within each waking moment. Anyone who trains in this path for a significant length of time will discover that the ability to perceive and understand is connected with their development and capacity on other levels, this brings around great improvements in life on all levels.

Question 4

⊙

For those who are starting out what encouragement would you offer to them?

Martin: The best advice I can give to anyone just starting their training, is to make sure their focus is completely clear and undivided. Your mission is to set up a constant training routine with which you fully understand and fully engage.

This may sound obvious, but, because to progress we must change and improve ourselves, we will come up against our shortcomings. This makes us uncomfortable and so of course, when we are uncomfortable we try to return to our previous state, the status quo. We often find all sorts of interesting barriers appear to diffuse, divide, distract or discourage us from continuing. This doesn't always appear in an overtly negative fashion. Sometimes this can come in the form of too much excitement, which leads to us attempting to follow multiple traditions and teachers and thus more than one very intense course of instruction at the same time. Often students will find that when they start to practice, they find themselves drawn to switch to something different just at the point where they are about to make progress. This is understandable because it is natural to look for an easier way of doing things. To find a different approach rather than transforming ourselves to meet that challenge. Sometimes we will even tell ourselves that the exercise we are doing is too easy, but yet we are failing to meet the criteria that is set forth before us.

Whatever form of distraction or barrier that appears, it is important to look at it so we can utilise this energy. Many people waste their energy on overthinking or talking about the path rather than practising it. Reading many different books has the same effect of diffusing their energy in many different directions. Make sure your focus is developing your own ability, not on self-expression, not on comparative religion, or the exploring of different cultures. Of course, we need to understand the underlying mechanism of what we are trying to do, and study is a very positive thing, but let's not let any other pursuit take up the energy that we really need to put into fully engaging in the challenges the path puts before us. Stick to the instructions given to you by the letter and make sure your sights are always set on the next achievement that you need to overcome to progress.

Question 5

⊙

For those who are seeking magical abilities what advice would you offer to them?

Martin: The abilities are natural side effects of your own evolution, they are very important and your desire for them is something you can use for great benefit and keep yourself motivated. Developing these abilities gives you the means to help those around you and to benefit the world. It is however, important to remember that to grow good fruit the focus needs to be on the tree itself, making sure that you water its roots, not the branches from which the fruits appear. The same is true on our path, focus on improving your abilities through exercises and these powers will come as nature takes its course and your path unfolds.

Question 6

⊙

What did you find was the most effective way in dealing with the soul mirrors?

Martin: To truly transform as a person you need to engage with the areas which you find hard in life. This often means moving outside our comfort zone and doing things we have never done before. When we find an area of life challenging often we build barriers that protect ourselves from facing those challenges.

Often we will devalue that skill or area of functioning and create elaborate reasons why we do not wish to improve ourselves in this area.

For this reason, it's important to be very honest, to look at your life objectively and open yourself up to what people around you are saying and what changes life is asking for you to make.

Our Hermetic exercises, of course, can very much help us as these involve improving all areas of our mental functioning. The key to success is to bring the skills and abilities you learn in your training into your normal functioning consciousness. Your magical training exercises are just that, they are training, which is to be used in every moment. In this way we move gradually to magical life. The more we develop the more fully we engage with each task. With time the practitioner will find themselves drawn to practice the things they find hardest in life, this is a sign that the soul mirrors are becoming balanced.

Question 7

⊙

What would you say for you was the most challenging aspect of this path for you and how did you conquer that challenge?

Martin: Aristotle was once asked, "What is the hardest thing for a human to master?" His answer was silence. From the Hermetic point of view, silence is a very important skill. It is for this reason, Franz Bardon notes repeatedly that a magician should not talk about his personal practice or progress unless to his teacher. The mastery of inner silence is directly linked to our ability to master the control of our words. A magician, therefore, should train both in tandem to gain self-mastery.

Question 8

⊙

When one speaks about being 'Enlightened', what in your opinion constitutes this state?

Martin: From the Hermetic point of view Enlightenment is a state of being in total harmony with all things.

Question 9

⊙

Could you please share with us what for you has been the most rewarding aspect of this journey?

Martin: It seems to me that all of us have our dreams and aspirations on life. For some this is material, they wish to live in beautiful surroundings, have positive people around them and do something to help the material world. Others seek intellectual knowledge like the historian who wishes to travel into the past or the scientist who wishes a clear vision of the underlying mechanisms of the universe. There are some like Enoch who longed to walk with the angels or Agrippa who wish to cultivate spiritual abilities to help his fellow man. I can honestly say that my training in the Franz Bardon system has brought all I have ever dreamed of and more. It has been the greatest blessing and most wonderful honour to practice.

Question 10

☉

How does one's experience change in Step eight and beyond?

Martin: *The Perfect Discourse of Hermes Trismegistus* states that either "all things are of God or all things are from God". In Hermetic training, all things are interconnected. Often you will find that gaining a new ability leads to a new understanding and vice versa. This can be seen in the *Corpus Hermeticum* where it is said that,

> *Just as the body once it has gained perfection in the womb goes out, likewise the soul, once it has gained perfection, goes out of the body...the perfection of the soul is the knowledge of what is.*

To start with the normal individual needs to develop himself and fully balance and integrate the elements within himself, only then are the later steps within his capability.

Question 11

☉

As a teacher of Hermetic meditation what are the main areas that students struggle with and why do you think this is so?

Martin: The beginning stages are usually the hardest. The first challenge is learning to maintain a constant training routine and for many, this is the greatest challenge they will face, as their internal barriers beset them from the outset. Within us all there are aspects of ourselves that are not fully directed towards our path. These can mean areas that have not yet developed the ability needed to engage with the training, or it can be aspects of the self that are injured and need to heal or recover. Sometimes emergency strategies or outmoded ways of doing things are hardest to break. Especially if the student has relied on a certain approach to life, so finds it hard to learn a new way of doing things. Have you ever known someone who won't do the one thing that will solve their problems? Often in life, they will mistake the medicine that will bring around their cure for poison.

The same is true of our internal aspects. These internal forces find various expressions to try to avoid the exercises which cause them discomfort, causing the student to become distracted, divided, redirected or disheartened. This leads to the student wanting to change the exercise, or give in and start something else, they would rather focus on anything other than the job in hand. It's the teacher's role to find a way to navigate this situation and to help each student recruit, redirect and reintegrate any internal objections so as to be able to fuel their further progress.

Question 12

☉

Could you please tell us more about your investigation into ancient Western Meditation research and how to become a patron?

Martin: In the modern-day we live in a kind of spiritual dark ages as far as our native western spiritual tradition is concerned. The man on the street is far more likely to know the sayings of Buddha than the teachings of Plato or Imhotep!

In ancient times we had a complete system of teachings with a wide range of methods of advancement. The temples would teach sacred gymnastics to balance and heal the body, and they handed down techniques of healing to correct the mind when things went wrong. We used to have our own traditions of breath control, lucid dreaming, opening the energy points on the spine and many more practices we no longer have access to. These traditions were recorded in ancient documents, but due to historical events modern practitioners have had to fill in gaps with oriental disciplines and traditions which have been more widely promoted. However, I believe that much of it is being rediscovered.

I propose that western civilisation will only regain its self-awareness when its spirit returns. When we once again restore and indeed live by the traditions our culture was built upon.

If you would like to see the techniques come back to life please visit my Patreon page to see the full schedule and to find out how you can get involved and lend your support.

Question 13

⊙

What do you feel ancient Western Meditation can offer?

a. What do you feel is missing from modern day practices?

Martin: Our ancient tradition had a very specific focus, to step beyond yourself and to become a living god. It was a beautifully joyful and expansive practice, which allowed you to step beyond yourself and grasp your higher nature.

In those days there was a dynamic and exciting Hermetic community working together to be in tune with everything good in the universe and to manifest this goodness on earth. This community had great value and protected practitioners from adversity, giving them a positive place and environment to grow in. The whole feel of the practice at that time was uplifting and evolutionary.

Question 14

☉

How can we benefit from these ancient teachings?

Martin: Our modern practice lacks understanding. We know what, but few of us know why. The ancient teachings cover far more in respect to how a path of development works, why we would be called to such a practice, what the purpose of life is and what role a magician takes in the great harmony of the universe.

Question 15

☉

How do these practices compare to Bardon's teachings?

Martin: Franz Bardon was a dedicated student of the Ancient Hermetic Teachings, something that becomes apparent to anyone who reads the Hermetica. Franz Bardon's works are the greatest technical guide to practical magical practice and leaves the philosophical outlook down to the individual. Those who feel a connection with the pure current of Hermeticism will find that ancient teachings compliment Bardon's path perfectly and bring an increased sense of celebration and inner harmony to their practice.

Question 16

⊙

Could you please explain to us more about the ancient origins of Hermetics from your research?

Martin: When Alexander the Great liberated Egypt from its Persian captors, two cultures with great wisdom and insight combined. The Magickal traditions of Ancient Egypt met with the philosophical traditions of Greece. The Greeks identified the Egyptian god of magic Thoth with their own messenger god called Hermes. History shows that the Egyptian priests allowed people of both genders and from all cultures and traditions to join what we now know as the Hermetic Order. In fact, it appears that although native Egyptian priests made up the majority of the order, they also had many Pythagoreans, Jews and Christians in their ranks.

Wanting to keep the hieroglyphs secret, they worked with Greek members of the order to translate the teachings into Greek texts, using the (then) modern philosophical style. A process you can see is happening again as many ancient teachings start to be described in psychological language, which is more acceptable in our day. During this process, something beautiful happened. The Egyptians knew the magical practices from both tradition and direct experiences, but the Greeks asked the questions and possessed the clarity to bring the underlying mechanisms of the path of spiritual evolution into focus. The alchemy between the two cultures have left us with great gifts, which are the texts we now possess.

Question 17

⊙

Please could share with us your future title Enlightened Living. What inspired you to write it and how do you feel it can benefit others?

Martin: During this interview, a few themes have appeared. The first being that the original focus of Hermetic practice was to become at one with the great good. To be in tune with and to express the underlying force of truth, light and goodness in the world.

The second being that Hermetic exercises do not a magician make. To truly take that role you need to take those skills and that mindset into every moment of your life, you need to live a magical life.

When you read *Enlightened Living* you will learn a set of very powerful methods, insights and observations that will allow you to bring these ancient Hermetic principles into your life. It will show you how to apply your magical powers to your daily life, to be able to fully express the principle 'as above so below' and make your life part of your magical training. In this way, it will aid you in overcoming plateaus in training and help you move forward in your path.

Chapter 7: Nenad Djordjevic-Talerman

Introduction

Nenad is an Honorary Vice President of the Royal Asiatic Society China in Shanghai. He lives in Shanghai where he is a freelance researcher, writer, tutor and musician. He had his first magical experiences as a child and he regards himself as Bardon's student.

He studied history in Stockholm and Belgrade and earned a master's degree in 1994. After working as a historian at the Yugoslavian archives, he joined the Ministry of Foreign Affairs in 1997. His diplomatic postings took him to Pyongyang in 2000, Beijing from 2002 to 2006, and Shanghai from 2006 to 2010. He is the published author of the *Old Shanghai Clubs and Association and Sapajou: The Collected Works of a Cartoonist. The Moon Zone co-authored by Kadyila Aili,* Falcon Books Publishing9, 2020 and *360 Heads of the Earth Zone: The First Step to Divine Providence Vol Spring*. Falcon Books Publishing, (2021).[10]
Nenad also has a Facebook Group called, 'Franz Bardon The Practice Magical Evocation.'[11]

9 https://amzn.to/3BvmKhR

10 https://www.thegreatbritishbookshop.co.uk/products/360-heads-of-the-earth-zone-the-first-step-to-divine-providence-volume-1-spring-1?_pos=1&_sid=9b15dcd71&_ss=r

11 https://www.facebook.com/groups/FranzBardonPractice

Questions & Answers

Question 1

⊙

Please could share aspects of your magical background and how your experiences as a child shaped your path?

Nenad: When I was a very small child, I remember how my guardian angel told me that I would not be able to see him anymore, and when I started to cry, he told me that he would always be around me and that I would be able to see him once again but much later in my life. When I was about four years old, I had a dream about fairies and gnomes, and when I woke up, they somehow transferred directly from my dream world into the physical reality, so for a few minutes, I saw them dancing in my room in their physical forms. About the same age, I was entirely shocked to realize that we all were going to die, and this perhaps is when my first spiritual quest began, as an attempt to understand if there really was a life after death.

I had a very nice childhood. I lived next to the oldest and most beautiful park in Belgrade, my hometown. I spent most of my time playing with friends, climbing trees and exploring ancient ruins and walls. We had our own magical trees which we adored. I strongly felt at that time that some secret paths did connect our world with other realities and that we could find actual portals hidden somewhere in the park. Those ideas were spontaneous. We had not heard about such things from anybody else nor read about similar things in any book. We were around seven or eight years old. Later, I understood that we had been actually worshipping nature and performing some kind of magic there as kids without knowing it or consciously wanting it.

Question 2

⊙

Were there any other influences in your life outside of Bardon's work that helped guide you along your spiritual path?

Nenad: The most influences have come from my family members – parents, sister, wife, sons; and closest relatives and friends. In my primary school, I was happy to have a very interesting biology teacher (whose family name happened to be the same as mine) whose lectures about biology were actually fascinating stories about the universe, lost civilisations, secrets of nature and all kinds of mysteries and magic. When I was fourteen years old I happened to buy a book about astral projection. It was in 1984. Such books were rare at that time. I was shocked to realise that astral projection was a real possibility for some people. There were a lot of instructions in that book about how to achieve astral projection and for two years I was practising very stubbornly almost every night and finally achieved my first conscious astral projection when I was seventeen. This book was surely one of the most influential in my life. Regrettably, I lost it. I even forgot the name of the author and the title. I have been trying to find this book on the internet, yet to no avail.

The next ten years after my first conscious astral projection, I had a lot of out of body experiences and saw a lot of spirits and different planes of existence. The problem was that I was very confused about the regions I was visiting. I was not sure what they were about and had little understanding of their nature and its inhabitants.

Various spiritual guides helped me a lot to gain a better understanding of it. I was also very lucky to find my human teacher – Tom de Liso, whose instructions and words of wisdom were very precious to me. He did his best to encourage my exploration of the Tree of Life and Thirty Aethyrs of Enochian magic. Thanks to Tom deLiso and his instructions I managed to visit all Sephirot in the Tree of Life where I was also blessed to meet archangels Sandalphon, Michael, Gabriel, Uriel, Raphael, Metatron and other great teachers and masters.

Question 3

☉

When did you discover Franz Bardon's writings and how did this change your practice?

Nenad: I do not exactly recall the date, but I guess it was around 2002, when I came to live in China, about the same time when I was taking a more serious interest in tarot, Yi Ying, teachings of old Christian gnostic schools and tantra. Some of my favourite authors from that time were also Omraam Mikhaël Aïvanhov, a great Christian Mystic and Gnostic and Robert Svoboda, who wrote a fascinating trilogy about Aghori and the life and teaching of his teacher, Vimalananda.

I started reading *Corpus Hermeticum* and became fascinated with hermetic tradition also. My studies of hermeticism, lead me finally to Franz Bardon. I was at once attracted to him a lot. I found it amazing how vast and detailed his knowledge was. I found his books very intelligently and spiritually written. I liked his personality too. Beyond all, he was a very good man.

I think that mostly due to his influences, as good as all Bardonian magicians I came in contact with are really good people as well. I had achieved my first conscious astral projection some fifteen years before I discovered Bardon's books, but Franz Bardon changed my practices in many different ways.

First of all, Franz Bardon's second book changed my perspective about evocations. I realised that even if I made progress in my out of body experiences, I had absolutely no idea how to perform an evocation. I might have seen some different realities in my out of body experiences, but I was never able to consciously evoke spirits into our world's reality. Thanks to Bardon, I have become interested in ceremonial magic. In one field, such as OBE (out-of-body experience), I felt advanced, but in other fields, such as evocation, I felt like a neophyte.

Question 4

⊙

Franz Bardon states:

> *To reach this maturity a certain pre-training is absolutely necessary. The reader will, therefore, find it natural that he must be fully conversant with the first tarot-card, at least up to Step 8, if he wants to have further positive success in his practice of higher magic"*

-The Magical Practice of Evocation

How important do you feel this statement is?

Nenad: Step 8 is about the separation of the mental body from the astral body, mental travelling throughout the universe, controlling the elements, influencing from the elements, preparation of fluid condensers and preparation of magical mirror. The magician who is able to achieve all of those things is undoubtedly very advanced. All previous 7 steps have helped the magician come up to that level, often after long and hard work. But once you get to that point, you will then also have it much easier to evoke and communicate with spirits and travel wherever you want around the universe.

When you astral or mental travel to different realities, you are a guest, but when you evoke to our physical reality, spirits are your guests. Step 8 helps you become a better host and guest. The magician who is about to master step 8 is also about to master both evocations and out of body experience (including astral and mental projection). The communication with spirits will be much easier from that point on, which all is much more explained in Bardon's second book on magical evocation. I often practised according to Bardon's instructions. And once you master one step, it does not mean you would never come back to it again. I always come back to Bardon's steps, especially to step 1. Nevertheless, before I discovered Bardon, I had been lucky to master astral and mental projections by my own efforts and later with the help of Tom de Liso. My point is that the magician can also come to step 8, by following other teachings and traditions.

You do not necessarily need to follow Bardon to reach Bardon's level of step 8. There are many different ways to come to this step. Franz Bardon gave only one example, but it is the golden example. I also noticed that many people take years to master some of Bardon's first steps. If they happened not to be able to move forward for years, maybe they could then take inspiration from some other books and teachers and later come back to Bardon again. If you have studied a magical tradition for thirty years and discovered Bardon for the first time when you are, let's say, sixty years old, I think that there is no reason that you should start your magical studies from the very beginning in order to reach the step 8, when you have actually already reached the level 8 by following some other traditions.

Question 5

☉

Could you tell us about the inspiration behind your up and coming title, 360 Heads of the Earth Zone: The First Step to Divine Providence. What can we expect from these Volumes?

Nenad: Let me quote Franz Bardon:

> *The size of this volume makes it impossible for me to give full details on each individual head; I can only publish a few words referring to the general facts of hermetic science...The description of many a head whose range of competence is very great would fill not just one volume, but a good number of volumes.*

The first time I was reading Franz Bardon I felt sorry that he omitted to write more details about the 360 heads of the Earth Zone and other spirits, but it also looked to me that with such remarks, he invited future magicians to continue his work. So, I felt a call to try to continue his work the best I could. So far I know, since Bardon's time, only three people focused their spiritual practices on the 360 heads of the Earth Zone: Emil Stejnar, William Mistele and Cynthia Schlosser. I would like to take this opportunity to acknowledge and offer my gratitude for their contribution on this subject. Nowadays, more people are interested in this area of Bardon's work. There are several great Franz Bardon groups online that cover Bardon's magic with a lot of interesting members.

I first started to evoke spirits from Bardon's book in 2006. In the next few years, I did my evocations sporadically but not in a systematic order. But in 2013 I decided to evoke all of them. I began my online journal on Friday, April 26, 2013, on Studio Arcanis, a magical forum, with the following sentences:

> *Well, I know their names, I know their sigils, I have seen and talked to some of them...But I am still not satisfied with my results. I want to see who they really are... So, I will dedicate my next year to working with the 360 heads of the Zone girdling the Earth... Since there are 360 heads, but 365 days in one year, I will more or less dedicate one day to each head of the Zone...*

My diary about evoking the 360 heads can still be read online,[12] (However, you need to be a member of Studio Arcanis in order to read it).

This book about *360 heads of the Earth Zone* includes some parts of this diary but also all of my previous and later evocations. It has taken me four years to write this book. During this time, I have evoked each of those 360 spirits at least two more times, if for no other reason, than just to confirm what I was writing about them was true.

In my description, each head of the Earth Zone contains the following elements: sigil; an alternative name which was used by Abramalin the Mage and Quintscher; Divine and angelic names for the circle and conjuration; dominant colour in space impregnation; number and colour of candles; the triangle arrangement; offerings; additional suggestions

[12] https://www.studioarcanis.com/viewtopic.php?f=33&t=8923

about evocation; similar spirits; the appearance of the spirit; the spirit's teachings and instructions; my experiences; the spirits' region; subordinate spirits; and possible problems and side-effects.

The second part of the title is, *The First Step to Divine Providence*. There are ten main steps to Divine Providence, and the first step is the Earth Zone. The second step is the Moon, the third step – Mercury, the fourth – Venus and so on. The last step is Kether.

My life aspiration is to write ten books about 10 steps to Divine Providence, but Divine Providence will also decide whether this will happen or not, because it is a huge task. I have finished two books about *The Moon Zone*[13](now available on Amazon) and *Mercury Zone* and I have gathered a lot of material about the Venus Zone too. But I am not doing this work alone anymore. It is too much for one person to handle, so these books are being written in collaboration with other magicians.

Question 6

⊙

With regards to Bardon's second title "The Magical Practice of Evocation," have you found that you have been drawn to work with EGZ Spirits more than others?

Nenad: The 360 heads of EGZ were the first group of spirits from Bardon's book which I explored systematically, but I have been also fascinated by working with spirits from all other planetary zones. The spirits of the Moon Zone are very mystical. The Mercurial spirits are extremely intelligent. The Venusians are pure souls and additionally very beautiful. The Martial spirits can be great protectors. We live on the Earth, so it is important not to neglect the 360 heads of EGZ even when we work with spirits from other planetary spheres. Nobody knows better our planet than the 360 Heads of EGZ, and they are willing to share their knowledge with us. They also want to help us properly understand our planet and our role in it, as long as we live here.

[13] https://amzn.to/2YUkxPb

Question 7

⊙

How have working with these beings assisted you in your daily life on practical level?

Nenad: I started systematically working with the 360 heads at the time when I decided to start something new in my life. First of all, they helped me overcome my personal "dark night of the soul" a crisis which came as a reflection of my crossing the Abyss. I was a successful diplomat but due to some personal reasons, I decided to leave the Ministry of Foreign Affairs and become a freelancer. It was a difficult decision. The 360 heads of the Earth Zone have been helping me in my aspiration to be a free man. They have helped me achieve financial stability. They are helping my family. Since I live in a foreign country, they assist me with local deities as well as with local communities and administration. Their influences are unmistakable.

Let me give you some examples. Kolani is an expert of occult dancing. I evoked Kolani for the first time in Shanghai in June 2013.At that time, I had no idea that I would just one month later make an unplanned trip to Konya (Turkey) where I also had the opportunity to visit Rumi's mausoleum, an old spiritual centre of Sufi's dancing. Pafessa, Abbetira, Siria, Giria, Alagill, Yraganon, Capipa, Jrmoni, Lurchi, Iserag, Aspadit and Nasi are related to financial matters. Due to their influences, I spent my first year after the first evocation of those spirits living and working in: Indonesia, Thailand, Burma, Turkey, China, and the Philippines.

My childhood dream was to become a rock singer, and thirty-five years later, this is exactly what I have become. It was totally unexpected. After my first evocation of Riqita, a head who is a guardian of singers. I evoked Baalto, a guardian of caves and underwater tunnels, and soon after I happened to see some of the most beautiful caves in the world in Guilin (China). Among other things, I am also a teacher, and I have been assisted by Zagriona and other spirits on daily basis. They also help me with writing. I have been healing some people with their help also. People now appreciate and like me for who I am, and not for my title and social or financial status, which is mostly due to their help. They also help me connect with nice people. They push me to work for peace in cooperation with some other magicians. They encourage me on my way to personal freedom. So far, not all of them were equally helpful, which is reasonable and normal. For instance, some of them are guardians of mathematicians, engineers and physicists. I am not good at those sciences and probably will never be, so I really do not expect to be assisted by them in those fields. But then again, who knows? Sometimes you need to wait for a while to be sure that you have observed their influences. If they all want to help at the same time, I would achieve all my dreams in one day, which is absurd and most probably unsurvivable.

Question 8

☉

When making the transition in IIH visiting the elemental realms and then moving on to the investigation of the 360 heads how does this change one's perspective on life?

Nenad: The 360 heads are teachers of 360 different faculties and 72 fields of magic. Their academies and temples are located in the Earth Zone. When people die, some of them will become their students. Among many other things, their students will learn there how to fly, become invisible, strive for peace, travel to other planets and help our humanity grow. One of the greatest things about the 360 heads is that we can be accepted as their students while we are still alive.

So, they help and teach us, but they also need us and sometimes they also need our help. They help our physical reality through us. The physical world needs to be taken care of and cultivated by us humans. This is our main role on this planet. If we neglect that role, then the 360 heads of the Earth Zone will not care to help us. The elemental realms help us understand nature and our role in it. They inflame our souls with love to all living beings. They also make us become more balanced and better human beings. That is all very important because if we do not strive to become better people, the 360 heads of the Earth Zone will just ignore us. We will never become a part of their company.

Question 9

⊙

Does working with these beings not only aid with bringing knowledge into this world, also what are the effects upon the mental body of the magician?

Nenad: Once upon a time, they were directly helping humanity grow in culture and sciences, but the stories from the three of Enoch's books remind us that the concept of their direct involvement in human affairs dramatically failed when the humans misused and misunderstood their knowledge.

Ever since that time, the great spirits have preferred to carry on the work of enlightenment through elected human beings. Franz Bardon used to say that some secrets are locked behind many locked doors for good reasons and can be revealed only to the mature magician.

Scientific discoveries may anew lead to world catastrophe. The heads of the Earth Zone know exactly that there are some big problems with human nature and that we have the potential to destroy the world we live in, so it is no wonder they are reluctant to help. Many spirits don't want to have any contact with immature people at all. Franz Bardon mentioned that many spirits are ready to reveal their teachings only to the magician with high ethical standards. All spirits whose faculty is to inspire inventors to new technical inventions reject to help the magician in any way, unless s/he is truly mature enough to receive such knowledge. And they have every right to be reluctant with all of those scientific experiments which have ended up with atomic bombs, chemical weapons and destruction of nature. So, the future of this humanity is left to the adepts which is the conscious decision of the Mercurial spirits. The adept needs to find a way how to approach spirits using his or her knowledge in magic, alchemy and astrology.

If they find the magicians worthy, they will help them strengthen their mental bodies with incredible proportions, but they would expect them to keep the sacred teachings from corruption and to keep up with the good work of the ancients with the aim to raise humanity up from its barbarous features to cultural heights.

With a strong mental body, we can travel to the end of the Universe where we can also by our own eyes witness the rays of creation. They can help us expand our memory and intellectual capabilities, so that we could remember all of our previous incarnations and understand what is behind a person even if we meet them for the first time and what is in the book after the first read sentence. We will be also lucid all the time if we wish. The only problem will be from then on how to find a way for people to understand you. Helping people is very difficult.

Question 10

⊙

With regard to the heads of the EGZ they are often spoken of as the true teachers of humanity, In your experience is this the case and how great an influence do they have upon our development?

Nenad: I think that I already partly answered that question, but let me add that if they like you then they can also teach you everything about anything which is related to our planet Earth. In their efforts to influence our development, the heads of the EGZ closely cooperate with the Mercurial spirits (Shem Angels).

Most of the 360 heads of the Earth Zone have a great affinity towards Mercury, but they use the Earth as a platform from where they teach and help human beings. Co-operations between Shem angels and heads of the Earth Zone are very intensive. Many heads of the Earth Zone have Mercurial characters and can teach the magicians a lot about Mercury mysteries. As they are also familiar with the human habit to abuse knowledge when they have a chance to do so, they now only elect trustworthy individuals to represent Mercurial affairs and interests upon the Earth. Those lucky persons are or will become: hermetic masters, advanced magicians, extraordinary alchemists, and outstanding astrologers–in other words–the true children of Mercury.

Question 11

⊙

In your work with these beings do you always evoke or meet within the EGZ and what is the reason for this?

There are different levels of EGZ. During the evocation, the spirits come to our world reality as our guests, and during our out of body experiences, we go there to their astral and mental realms to be their guests. They sometimes follow us to Akasha. One and the same spirit after their appearance in our world's reality may suggest to guide you to the realms where they live. I personally think that the mutual visits between you and a spirit you have evoked is a sign of the most successful evocation. In my experience, the meetings with spirits are as real as anything else from our world's reality when they happened in the astral region. When they come to our world's reality during the evocation, they most often appear in their etheric forms. They are observable and you can communicate with them, but you need to be lucid and at least slightly influenced by their energy. But the evocation is always magical and if it is successful you will already find the best way of communication with the evoked spirit spontaneously. When they are in our world's reality, most often they are in the etheric plane, which is the densest part of the astral region, which also means that we need to raise our consciousness just a bit in order to see them properly.

Some heads of the Earth Zone teach about other planets. So, it can also happen that they decide to guide us to Mercury, Venus, the Sun or other planetary spheres. For example, when I evoked Bekaro for the first time, I spent a few hours with him on Mars, which I did not expect at all because I thought he was to teach me about the fire element. Bekaro introduced me there to some Martial spirits. In the end I learned something, there about the fire element but from Mars' perspective.

Question 12

With regards to the preparation of the magic circle in evocation, Bardon offers a number of examples of how this can be performed. How best would you advise someone to prepare the magic circle for the first time?

Nenad: Franz Bardon required from us the perfect understanding of the magic circle, but was quite flexible about how we can use it. I can speak here only about my personal experiences. If you evoke a spirit for the first time, draw a circle around you with chalk. Write inside the circle related to Divine names and archangels. The same names you write in the circle, you will also mention in your conjurations. In my book, I suggest related Divine names and names of archangels for each of the 360 heads of the Earth Zone. It is important to have them included within the circle, not so much because of protection, but more in order to attract their attention. We do not want to attract some random spirits during our evocations. If you invite your friend for a visit, you most probably would not like to be visited by an unknown person from the street who is also pretending to be your friend. Some spirits like to fake their identity for one reason or another.

Besides the circle, it is very important to have the right sigil. In later evocations of the same spirit, you will most probably not need to draw a physical circle on the floor around you anymore, but you will always need to have the right sigil. The sigil is the ancient sign of recognition. The spirit might not hear your conjuration, but he will know that you want to see him once he observes his sigil by your side. And always do remember to light the candle, at least when you evoke inside.

Question 13

⊙

How important do you feel understanding the symbology of the circle and triangle is in order to perform evocation successfully?

Nenad: I think that Franz Bardon perfectly explained the meaning of the circle and triangle. And he also asks us to have a perfect understanding of both in order to have successful evocations. Related to the triangle, some rules should be applied no matter if we have it visualised or physically drawn on the floor. The triangle is the place where the spirit is going to appear in your room as your guest, so try to make it large and comfortable. The heads of the Earth Zone are mighty spirits, so you cannot really expect them to feel nice if you arranged for them a few inches' wide triangle. Probably, they will ignore you and think that you are disrespectful. If they still agreed to come, they would then for sure ignore your triangle altogether and sit somewhere else. In my book, I suggested special triangle arrangements and offerings for each of the 360 heads. 'As above-so below': try to treat your head the same way as you would treat your human friend. Offer them a chair to sit in and at least a glass of water.

Question 14

⊙

I wonder if you could share with us your first experience of performing magical evocation and how did it differ from working with the elemental realms?

Nenad: Elementals are truly fantastic creatures. Their kings and queens are for example are the best experts of their related elements. So, if you want to learn something basic about the water element, the best option would be then to ask some undines for help. Many of them are incredibly sensitive. I am often afraid that I might accidentally hurt them when I see them. One of them, a water spirit, told me that she was not happy. When I asked her why not, she said that she only had three marbles, while her girlfriend had more than ten. They can share many innocent stories like that. They are very playful and pure souls.

There are all possible kinds of salamanders. Some of the tiniest are attached to the candle flames. They are eager to act especially when the candles are used in the love magic rituals. Some fiery spirits are very mighty. Malacha can, for example, help the magician become a friend with a powerful royal family of fiery dragons. One of the most important fiery spirit is Aftif, a high priest of the Fire Temple, who has a very friendly attitude towards human beings and some human priests are under his supervision. Lurchi has a very joyful company of subordinate spirits who are representatives of the most carefree and pleasurable aspects of the fire element.

They live in a very romantic region of the Earth Zone. Lurchi's settlements are frequently visited by other spirits, not only because of their beauty. By mere walking through Lurchi's fields, they would immediately regain additional sources of energy and vitality.

The Eight important sylphs are mentioned by Franz Bardon: Parahim, Apilki, Erkeya, Dalep, Capisi, Drisophi, Glisi, and Cargoste. Franz Bardon acknowledged that he had not had much success with them, so he suggested evocations of the heads whose faculty was the air element instead.

On the other hand, it is known that Paracelsus, Socrates, Psellos, Abbé de Villars, Benvenuto Cellini and some other people from the present and past managed to make friends with sylphs. For instance, Cellini wrote in his diary that his favourite art model was a very beautiful sylphide. When you see sylphs, try to relax and enjoy their quickness, intelligence and unpredictability. You will typically become first aware of them when you hear their silvery voices. Pay them respect, show friendly feelings to them and state what you would like to get from them. They can help you write poetry, teach you about other arts, give you the gift of prophecy and make you capable to look into the minds of other people.

The magician can evoke gnome kings in the name of Adonai Ha-Aretz and Adonai Melek, Shemhamphorash angels Elemiah and Hahasiah and archangels Uriel and Sandalphon. You may also recite the Prayer of the Gnomes from Levi when you evoke a gnome king. You need to introduce yourself to gnome kings, build a relationship with them and spend time learning about their kingdoms before you go asking for favours. Gnome kings are often very melancholic. They don't talk much, but they are very wise. Gnomes and Dwarves under them are very close to us, they are truly earthy creatures. They can help you learn to take care of your finances and other material goods. King Ghob is probably the most famous gnome king. His supreme reagent on the angelic level is Phorlakh. A few gnome kings are also mentioned by Franz Bardon: Mentifil, Ordaphe, Orova, Idurah, Musar, Necas, Erami, and Andimo.

Question 15

⊙

Did it meet your expectations?

Nenad: If you want to expand your understanding of the four elements, it is best then to cooperate with both elementals and related heads of the Earth Zone and other planetary spheres. Let me start with the fire magic.

The following heads of the Earth Zone are responsible for the fire magic:

1. Morech (1° Aries) – active, impulsive and extreme knowledge
2. Malacha (2° Aries) – the fire element on different planes
3. Kosem (1° Leo) – fire in the Earth Zone
4. Aluph (1°Scorpio) – fire on the physical plane of the Earth
5. .Bekaro (22° Aries) – salamanders
6. Molabeda (2° Taurus) – secrets of nature and sex
7. Nudatoni (2° Cancer) – volcanoes and earthquakes
8. Serap (1° Taurus) – passion
9. Lurchi (4° Aries) – love and wealth
10. Galago (12° Taurus) – impregnation of aura
11. Tabbata (10° Leo) – Invulnerability, especially against the fire

There are a number of heads of the Earth Zone who are great teachers of water magic. They help the magician become: successful in love, become a great healer, have safe journeys on water, control the sea life and enjoy the company of the most marvellous water spirits.

The following heads of the Earth Zone are related to the water magic, their more precise faculties are as follows:

1. Elami (30° Sagittarius) – underground waters
2. Tabori (10° Aries) – secrets of the water element
3. Hahadu (20° Aries) – undines
4. Sapasani (30° Taurus) – sea salt
5. Hyris (19° Aries) – magic of water and undines
6. Hipogo (20° Virgo) – ships
7. Horasul (29° Scorpio) – water regulation
8. Calamos (29° Taurus) – sea life
9. Merki (28° Libra) – fishing
10. Seneol (30° Gemini) – water-sports
11. Dimurga (10° Sagittarius) – travel on water
12. Irmano (30° Scorpio) – controlling water animals
13. Anadi (28° Scorpio) – hydrotherapy
14. Calacha (30° Aries) – hydrotherapy
15. Megalogi (30° Libra) – medical springs
16. Andrachor (29° Leo) – magical water
17. Caraschi (10° Scorpio) – medical magnetism

The magician can learn a lot about air magic from the following heads of the Earth Zone:

1. Kagaros (7° Leo) – mediatory principle of air
2. Pliroki (6° Cancer) – message through the air
3. Barnel (17° Aries) – love and music through the air element
4. Magelucha (18° Taurus) – mastering the air and water
5. Romasara (8° Leo) – pranayama

The following heads of the Earth Zone are related to the earth magic:

1. Nadele (24° Aries)
2. Baalto (25° Taurus)
3. Amia (18° Capricorn)
4. Kamual (19° Capricorn)
5. Yromus (25° Aries)

The heads of the Earth Zone are very friendly and they can teach the magicians all that they would like to know about: gnomes, finding lost things, crystals and precious stones, mining, and earth in ceremonial magic and alchemy. They inspire us to laugh and have a good time. To entertain our friends with great jokes, give away gifts; make some money. To learn how to save and invest and take care of ecology. Help gnomes in their hard work to preserve our planet; cultivate friendship with our crystals and stones and communicate with the suit of Pentacles in tarot. They are closely related to archangel Uriel, who is the guardian of the earth element and the master behind secrets of manipulating the matter, and who sometimes appears as a large beam of purple light.

Question 16

Is there anything else you would like to add?

Nenad: The 360 heads cover many different fields of magic from the Earth Zone including: the four elemental forces, nature, stones, flora, fauna, agriculture, food, family, education, literature, love, sex, healing, music, sciences, religion, technology, inventions, art, weather, justice, virtues, alchemy, phenomenal magic, entertainment, wealth, karma, astral magic, mental magic, Akasha, Divine Providence, etc. Each field of magic consists of many different subjects. All in all, the heads of the Earth Zone can teach humans about 1,500 different subjects altogether. Some subjects are similar to the ones from our world's reality, but others are quite different. The beauty of being a magician is that we can attend their schools, learn their subjects and pass their exams while we are still alive. The heads of the Earth Zone do not hide information, but can sometimes give it under the seal of secrecy.

I hope that one day people will get to know them better. This world would become a much better place if there were more people willing to cooperate with them. They will surely give you knowledge and skills, but they will also expect you to be a better human being and do your best to help humanity grow.

If I may suggest to our readers something at the end. Be humble. Do not show off with your knowledge. They will help you find some amazing information about your origin. You may become a member of their family. Maybe you will realise that you are closely connected to Olympian gods, Cherubim angels or some other mighty groups of spirits. But even if that was the case, do not tell that to other people. It is your secret. Do not say that you are more special than other people. See yourself as an ordinary human being. Do not compare with others. You are no crystal parent nor indigo child. Be normal. If you do not cultivate normal human virtues, the heads of the Earth Zone won't bother to meet you. They will just ignore you. And be careful with your new powers and learn how to control them!

In the end, I would like to thank you Tanya for your great work in spreading knowledge and wisdom in the world.

CHAPTER 8: RAY DEL SOLE

INTRODUCTION

Ray del Sole has been a Franz Bardon practitioner for over twenty years. He is known as an expert in metaphysics and mysticism and is an author of a series of books about spiritual development and training. Besides webinars, he also provides workshops and lectures in German-speaking countries and in England and in the USA. Ray works in Germany, near Frankfurt, as a Naturopath in Psychotherapy and as a Spiritual Healer. He is the founder of SURA Academy[14] where he takes students through a step by step program in spiritual development.

His focus lies in the application of hypnotherapy, past-life therapy, and Pranic Healing. His previous studies include.
Architecture in Bochum with a focus on Project Management, Cultural Training, General Project Management, Business Efficiency, Business Management for Engineers, Moderation of Working Groups. A Postgraduate in the Natural Sciences in Eco-Biology at the Institute Neubeuern, and Management Theory and Business at the University of Applied Sciences in Darmstadt. After several years as an Architect, he left the building industry for health reasons.

Since he had very early already undergone a complete education in Prana Healing in Switzerland, and because of his intensive spiritual studies in psychology and healing, he then completed the following training in Anxiety and Stress Management. Including a Psychological Counsellor, Hypnotherapist, Reincarnation Therapist, Hypno-coach, and a Medical Practitioner in Psychotherapy. He is a member of VFP (Association of Independent Psychotherapists in Germany).

[14] https://sura-academy.com/

Questions & Answers

Question 1

⊙

Please could you tell us about yourself and how you came across Bardon's IIH?

Ray: Originally I studied architecture. But now I have my own psychotherapy and coaching practice. Here I can help people by combining spiritual knowledge and healing techniques as well as the professional psychotherapy approach. Altogether it is a wonderful holistic way to cause real changes for my clients in a very effective way.

Modern psychotherapy lacks spiritual knowledge, especially the knowledge of the occult anatomy and the application of energies to dissolve blockages and to allow for real healing to take place. So this is a great experience for me to work in this way.

I must say that I was always driven by the idea to gain real wisdom. This idea was already very strong when I was a young boy at primary school. I decided to dedicate myself to this aim, willing to sacrifice other things which are normally important in life. Later in high school, I was able to study many different areas of knowledge such as science, religion and ancient history, I had the insight it was important for me to study the "whole world" if I wanted to really understand the "whole world" as it is. And this idea I have followed.

On my path, I have researched many different philosophies and spiritual schools, always with the idea to serve mankind for making progress.

When I was around eighteen years old, I visited an esoteric exhibition, just for fun to check what the people were offering. And here I discovered Bardon's first book. The German title suggested that this book was an instruction to become a real adept and this made me curious. So I have read the description on the back cover. I was astonished to read that Bardon was offering instructions for magical development. At the time it was quite uncommon, something special. So far I had only bad negative associations about magic as I heard many stories of magicians who did strange things creating bad results, or at best were quite mysterious. But when I was scrolling through the book, I was even more astonished about the scientific way Bardon gave exercises and explanations. I was so fascinated that I really wanted to know what he was talking about and if all these mysteries about magicians were true. And so, that day my path began. I have devoured his book, diving deeper and deeper into this magical world. Over the years, I have compared his teachings with the teachings from other spiritual traditions and I have also acquired greater knowledge to further my understanding and his core teachings. After many years of study and practical training, I must say that I am more than grateful for having taken this very special path. There are indeed so many uncountable treasures waiting for the student. Bardon gives all the keys to open the doors."

Question 2

⊙

You have mentioned in the past there is a wise way to approach Bardon's and a slow way: Please could you expand upon this and What would you advise someone who is starting out?

Ray: Bardon has written all his books with a secret wink. He offers official instructions which work like a route description. But you can read also between the lines and then you discover smart ways to get from A to B. These "secrets" can be found by real practical training and deep studies of all his books. Further on, the additional knowledge of the occult anatomy regarding the psychic centres, the chakras is a big deal for progress. And certainly, the subconsciousness can be integrated into the training very well. Bardon is a real master in giving small hints to big and important topics and he leaves it up to the student to become aware of these hints and to follow them. He simply assumes that the mature student will manage his way independent from problems, obstacles, etc.

Besides these "secrets" or a smart way to do the training, it is fascinating that the whole training system is so simple that it can be accomplished also without comprehensive intellectual studies. This means that you could take the book and give it to a young man who has no education at all but who has a great desire for spiritual mastery and this young man would just have to follow stubbornly the single exercises. For sure, he would reach mastery in the end. All is given in the exercises and in short explanations. It takes only motivation and stubbornness to go through it. Simplicity is the key and later these developed skills will help you understand what you are doing. And this shows the problem which we have to face today: We are used to dealing with complexity, with complex problems and complex solutions. We are not used to simplicity but simplicity is the nature of all real spiritual teachings. God is simple as God is the One while creation itself is based on diversity, on big numbers and with this on complexity. Those who want to understand God must learn simplicity. We move from the complex world of creation to the top of the pyramid, the One to experience unity.

In fact, our problem is the approach. We try to manage all challenges with the intellect but the intellect plays a minor role here. Intuition is holistic and practical experiences are most important. The intellect is too limited for all the wonders of the magic-mystical path and real spirituality. To answer both questions at once: I would suggest to the beginner to study deeply all books of Bardon and to implement quite early very important knowledge, such as his teachings on wisdom and the laws of creation. Further on it is very important to follow all hints, even if he mentions only a word or half of a sentence. In the main, this is the occult knowledge of the chakra system and the comprehensive use of the subconsciousness right from the start. Different techniques should be combined and orientated on realizing one aim. And in fact, one of his biggest "secrets" is that he simply expects the student to have a spiritual-mystical attitude together with good health. So if you suffer from imbalances of the mind, soul or body, then these are obstacles on the path. And without a truly spiritual attitude, you have the best chance to fall into the countless traps of selfishness and delusions which are waiting on both sides of the narrow path.

Only having a spiritual attitude can offer real safety and good progress. Having a mystical attitude means that you love God, that you long for divine unity, that you are willing to refine yourself and to serve mankind and creation. Only when you understand yourself as a part of the greater whole, all other parts (beings) are willing to support you as you do it. Creation means cooperation. We are all serving each other. Selfishness is an illusion. It simply does not work out.

Unfortunately, Bardon does not emphasize the importance of the spiritual-mystical attitude directly in his first book but talks only much later about these things and simply assumes that everyone knows it. In fact, what Bardon calls magic is pure spirituality in its highest form. We all have to walk the path of metaphysics and mysticism independent from culture and tradition.

Question 3

☉

In step 2 of IIH Bardon discusses working with the subconscious mind. In your opinion what is the best approach in dealing with this?

Ray: Bardon often shows a fascinating way of accessing topics. I guess that most students directly step into the trap of the "evil" subconsciousness blocking progress and supporting all that we don't want. This can develop into a real fight with the subconsciousness and cause lots of problems. One main point to understand is that if you have a strong Will, you won't experience any problems with your subconsciousness. The subconsciousness only sabotages your wishes if you lack willpower. And already by undergoing the concentration exercises, you will develop a good and strong Will. Then there is also a secret in it. You can bring your Will and your subconsciousness into the same positive state where both cooperate. The Will or normal consciousness can be seen as the male pole and the subconsciousness can be understood as the female pole. Our wishes are, seeds planted by the Will and carried out by the subconsciousness. The subconsciousness in its female power is completely underestimated. So indeed, active training should go hand in hand with the use of the subconsciousness to enable new abilities, to grow (overnight). I have written a book on this topic so everyone can apply the techniques of autohypnosis professionally.

Lastly, it is very important to realize a loving and positive unity with your subconsciousness and to neglect the idea of fighting it as this takes up a lot of energy and only causes problems.

Question 4

⊙

As a practitioner of Hypnosis, how have you found your work aided those practising Bardon's IIH?

Ray: The name 'hypnosis,' is simply another term for working on the subconsciousness, using states of trance. We can say that hypnosis consists of using techniques of mental magic and meditation and working on the Akashic level, If the hypnotist is skilled enough then he can work with energies to enable healing and revitalising, including the dissolving of blockages. Also, to mental travel with his clients beyond time and space. It is not uncommon to go into former incarnations for research and healing and to meet with spiritual guides and deceased souls.

In conclusion, hypnosis is magic and magic includes hypnosis. There are no real limits. The main use is certainly focused on healing and the analysis of the root of the problem, but also new skills and qualities can be anchored and strengthened in a person. These techniques are all very fascinating. For this reason, I recommend to all my students that they study psychotherapy and hypnotherapy because you can learn a lot about magic, and is also rewarding in this sense.

Hypnosis can be also seen as a guided meditation, when you meditate in a deeper state then you do something like autohypnosis already. The focus of hypnosis is the inner experience contrary to the outer experience of the material world.

So indeed we work on the higher planes. And in the subconsciousness, we find not only the roots of all problems but also the individual solutions. The subconsciousness is connected to the whole of creation on all planes.

Question 5

⊙

Following on from Question 4, which tools can you recommend students use in the early stages of IIH?

Ray: I recommend understanding the principles of autohypnosis and applying specific anchors using hand postures and finger postures. It is easy to find a good book about autohypnosis to understand the main principles. Then you can begin by sitting in your armchair, the same one which you use for your meditation or your concentration exercises. This way you can program your subconsciousness with the idea that every time you sit in your armchair, your body is calm while your mind enters into the perfect state for meditation. All outer disturbances will be automatically ignored so that you can accomplish your exercises perfectly. Indeed you can use this method of sitting in your armchair for all of your exercises. This would be called, an "armchair anchor."

Further on, you could think about different postures using your hands or fingers like the known mudras where you connect certain states of consciousness or where specific powers are activated. This is a fascinating field of experimentation where you can follow your intuition.

The more routines and programs you "install," the better can your subconsciousness support you. For example, use the same time, the same place and the same posture, then all you need for a specific exercise will be offered automatically.

Question 6

⊙

In your book The Path of The Mystic, you offer guidance to those who wish to follow a devotional/mystical path can integrate that along with Bardon's IIH practice. For the beginner, Could you please tell us a bit more about this title what inspired you to write it?

Ray: Bardon says that IIH deals with magic and yes, certainly this is the case. Magic is nothing else than metaphysics, by this I mean the science of physics on the level of mind and soul. Working with energies and corresponding laws. Bardon emphasizes the importance that magic and mysticism have to go hand in hand if the student does not want to suffer from any imbalances (or problems).

This idea to combine the teachings and training of metaphysics with the idea of cleaning, healing and refinement of mysticism is a matter of wisdom and with this of the fourth Tarot Card respectively, higher teachings. Here we see how important it is to read all books before starting the training of IIH respectively. Bardon mentions this problem jin only in one or two sentences in IIH. Besides this, the training of IIH can appear at least in parts as really dry and hard as it lacks all the beauty of normal spiritual teachings which are a matter of mysticism, the quality aspect of the whole training and development.

Mysticism gives life to the dry training. It also offers motivation, happiness, a real sense in all the training. The mystic loves God, loves mankind and creation, loves to serve, loves to refine himself and to unite with God. Love is a great drive, a great motivation. And devotion and humbleness have much greater meanings than most people understand. In the end, real mysticism is a matter of the third book about the cosmic language. Here you understand that the highest mystical practice means to transform your nature to the macrocosmic divine nature in all aspects. So a real mystic is the highest authority in creation. Only a real mystic can create as God creates.

I try to offer the student some mystical teachings to compensate for the magical training, to make it more vital and fascinating, also emphasising aspects of cleaning, healing and refinement which can never be overrated. Especially, beginners often have to face many problems simply because they have too many mental and emotional blockages which need to be cleaned, dissolved, so that healing can take place and on this level of higher harmony success is easier to accomplish. For this reason, I emphasize a lot in many of the steps the use of cleaning, healing and refinement in my Academy (SURA) and in my books. "Cleaning, healing and spiritualization (refinement)!" was the slogan of the old mystics,

> *Only those who are refined to divine degrees can unite with God.*

Question 7

⊙

Would be willing to share your own experience of the mystical path with us?

Ray: I guess if I wanted to share all my mystical experiences I would have to write a new book. Mystical experiences can be understood as states of unity with the Divine in one, or several aspects which come along with trance and great feelings of a diversity of ecstasies. The unity with God makes you feel really high, beyond normal human experiences and you take part in divine virtues and powers. These are all experiences of the highest fulfilment.

I must admit that this is not my first incarnation where I worked on my spiritual development, so my path might look a little bit different. While normally the student undergoes a long training before experiencing the Divine, I have more or less directly started with the experience of divine unity. I remember sitting in the backseat of my parent's car, driving somewhere. I would practice the stillness of mental exercise and then I got the insight that already through this exercise one could accomplish enlightenment just for the reason that a vacuum cannot exist in nature and if your mind is empty then something else can enter – the Divine

Spirit. This realization gave a kind of first enlightenment where my crown chakra was activated and bigger streams of energy were running through me. Not much later, I had the idea to listen to music where the sound "E" was emphasized. I started to sing "eeeeeee" by myself and I got into a very devotional attitude, praising God and expressing my love and my longing for divine unity. This manifested a lot of dark violet light, flooding my whole energy system and breaking up my skullcap. It felt like a massive waterfall of the highest energies falling on my head, into my head, flooding everything. Since that time I have had a big bump on my head where the energies were so strong that my physical skull transformed. The waterfall feeling lasted several days and afterwards I was not the same as before. The cosmic impersonal consciousness was installed in which has since been a part of me.

It was only many years later that I understood what had happened. I had performed the Kabbalistic letter "E" without consciously knowing it. This cosmic letter has the quality of cosmic consciousness. This means that I had already in a former incarnation trained in the cosmic letters, and Kabbalistic teachings. At the time, I was still a teenager. Much later, I underwent Bardon's Kabbalistic training and I must say that it is so full of beauty that one can feel very blessed to be allowed to experience it. Nothing makes me happier than God. The whole mystical training with all the offered ecstasies and wonderful experiences is beyond human understanding as we have here nothing whatsoever could serve in comparison. As always, you have to taste the fruits by yourself.

QUESTION 8

⊙

WHAT ADVICE AND GUIDANCE WOULD YOU OFFER TO THOSE FOLLOWING IIH?

Ray: In short: take care of your balance, your vitality. Get rid of all blockages and imbalances as early as possible, Cultivate a positive spiritual attitude and mystical love and devotion. Keep things simple. Don't waste time on stupid and selfish discussions on the internet. Don't waste your precious time on losing yourself in pure intellectual studies.

Real training is most important. Not a single book can replace real exercises.

Pay respect to all aspects of life. Find like-minded fellows on the path. Lonely wolves are lonely, but not more successful or happier than a group of students. Don´t do stupid things. Always have the four pillars of the temple of Solomon in mind. Try to understand the keys of wisdom, the laws of creation as early as possible. Be a positive example to the world and your fellowmen. And certainly, follow your higher intuition. Pray a lot for guidance and the power to manage all your challenges. Express your love and gratitude towards God. Be open to all the good and all the gifts which are waiting for you. Do good deeds. Serve well! And maybe join me at SURA Academy[15].

Question 9

⊙

How would you explain the books of Franz Bardon to someone who has no understanding of magic but is a spiritual seeker?

Ray: When you look only at the facade, then it seems that Bardon´s first book deals with the training in magic, the second book deals with the evocation of spirits and the third book deals with the training in Kabbalah. But this is only the superficial impression.

In fact, Bardon offers holistic, well-balanced training corresponding to universal standards and the highest knowledge that can be applied by every true spiritual seeker independent of his culture, religion or tradition. It is really the first time that the universal teachings were presented to the public in such a way and further on for self-initiation. With the given keys for development, the seeker can realize the Divine nature in all aspects and will further on getting to know the whole creation and its administration. I could not have been presented in an anymore straightforward way, everything else is just a matter of progress by training. Indeed we can say that Bardon offers the map for God,

15 https://sura-academy.com/

creation and the human being for a safe journey and a lawful development.

Behind the terms of Magic, Mysticism, Evocation and Kabbalah, where purest spirituality is hidden. It is all about the real and purest path of spiritual development while names and terms are quite secondary. To explain:

— Magic has the meaning of physics, the science of physics on the level of mind and soul. Physics deals with the different energies in quantity and quality and the corresponding laws.
— Mysticism deals with all the aspects of quality, refinement, healing and development. When you deal with energies or powers, then you must necessarily also deal with the question of quality, of intention and purpose. Mysticism can be seen as another term for true spirituality, for loving God and longing for unity.
— Evocation is a big term but in fact, the book simply explains the composition of the administration of creation, our solar system with the spheres and spirits (angels). Creation cannot work without intelligence, without laws and these divine beings the magician gets to know. These are indeed the great teachers of mankind, those who inspire people on earth to accomplish progress and new inventions.
— Kabbalah is just a traditional term for the cosmic language, the language of God, the Divine Spirit who creates with it all the worlds on all planes. The cosmic language contains the primordial components of creation. Everything is made of the cosmic language out of nothing, out of Akasha, the state of energy beyond creation.

This all means that you have the chance to accomplish your highest spiritual development when you follow Franz Bardon teachings beyond human terms. The cosmic language can be also understood as the science of chemistry corresponding to the science of physics regarding magic.

It is important to understand that Bardon has chosen a specific system to present his teachings. Imagine you would have to write instructions about how all the secrets of the world, of creation, of God, of the human being, of the administration and of the way you should take to experience everything in a safe and well-balanced way. Then you would have to ask yourself how you could accomplish this task. There are certainly many possibilities. Bardon has decided for himself to follow an old and also universal system of initiation which is reflected by the so-called Tarot Cards. Every card contains special teachings about a specific field. The first card deals with the initiation into magic, the second with evocation, the spiritual hierarchy or administration, the third with the cosmic language, the fourth with wisdom, and so on. This system follows an inner logic and higher sense. But it cannot adapt itself to the present needs of the individual seeker. It describes the ideal path of initiation and it is up to the seeker to study it with a focus on his individual needs. For this reason, I have already pointed out that it makes sense to study all books before starting the practical training and to integrate as early as possible the teachings of wisdom.

At last – all books contain so much information, so much precious knowledge and countless hints for further research that it is highly recommendable to read the books over and over again to get all the details.

> *There are no higher teachings available on earth, a training system which is perfectly balanced to accomplish real mastery in a most efficient way.*
>
> ~ *Initiation Into Hermetics,* Franz Bardon

Question 10

☉

As the founder and teacher of Sura Academy, could you tell us a bit about how the Academy approaches IIH and what can people expect when they join?

Ray: I have spent a lot of time conducting research, studies and experiments. From my point of view, it is not necessary for everyone to take the path of a lone-wolf, facing all kinds of questions and problems alone and spending too much time and effort to solve them. I think that it makes much more sense to walk the path together and help each other by sharing precious knowledge and experiences. This saves a lot of time and headache, while it makes the training efficient, easier and better in the results. Additionally, it offers very precious experiences of brotherhood and friendship internationally. When I think of all these great souls which I have met already and with whom I am walking the holy path for many years already, then I feel deep gratitude and much love.

From these thoughts of helping each other, sharing experiences and the high values of true spiritual friendship, the idea of an own academy was born several years ago. But for a single person, it is not easy to realize, such as forming an academy and so it took time to form. Meanwhile, we have plenty of teaching material. I am especially happy that we are able to offer holistic training including healing sessions, coaching and many other beneficial forms of support. This means we are also able to focus on the mystical aspects of the training as well as the magical. Both mystical practices and magical practices go hand in hand. In the future, we will have also a series of videos with guided meditations to support the exercises in the training and I will also offer education in spiritual healing. Everything is in wonderful progress.
Those wishing to join SURA Academy will have successfully passed the entrance test. In general, have a truly spiritual attitude which is needed since we do not support any unhealthy, selfish or dark ideas. We are dedicated to the highest ideals and this also means that we feel like a spiritual family of brothers and sisters.

All true spiritual seekers are welcome!

Question 11

⊙

Is there anything else you would like to add?

Ray: Thank you, Tanya, for the interview! And thank you very much for all the good work you do to support our fellow practitioners on this Holy Path!

CHAPTER 9: VIRGIL

INTRODUCTION

Treating others with kindness is the first magical act the magician learns and the last one he masters.

~Virgil

Virgil is a writer and Christian magician who has worked extensively with Franz Bardon's system of magic and enjoys sharing his insights through various outlets. He is currently the author of four books –*The Spirit of Magic*, *The Elemental Equilibrium*, and *The Covert Side of Initiation, The Gift to be Simple* – and runs the blog, 'Living Franz Bardon.'[16]

Although he enjoys sharing his insights, he enjoys encouraging others to share theirs even more. For this reason, during the summer of 2019, Virgil organized the first Franz Bardon community fundraiser, which resulted in the publication of the collaborative book '*Equipoise: Insights into Foundational Astral Training.*' This book is a compilation of essays and poems about magical equilibrium written by over two dozen students and initiates of Franz Bardon's system, and profits from its sales go to the 'Best Friends Animal Society.'

Virgil believes that who a magician really is, depends on his or her level of compassion, kindness, and forgiveness. According to Virgil, magical skills, psychic abilities, and occult knowledge can never substitute for these three traits, but aspiring magicians, in their rush to explore the Greater Mysteries, often lose sight of this basic spiritual fact.

Many of Virgil's writings are intended to remind readers that one cannot be a good magician without first being a good person, and that at the end of the day any form of power, including magical power, is of no value unless one has the wisdom needed to use it for the purposes of love.

[16] https://livingfranzbardon.blogspot.com/

Although he is able to write about the technical aspects of magic, Virgil rarely does so, opting instead to produce writings that help aspiring magicians keep sight of the things that truly matter.

QUESTIONS & ANSWERS

High Steps by a Yellow Bridge by Virgil

While descending stairs,
Terror grips my heart and vision.
I am bound to a weathered railing,
And slower than an ambling turtle.
This is my ball and chain.
You are fearless.
Walking as if on flat land,
You glide ahead – lower and lower.
My birth keeps me from reaching you,
And asking you your favorite season.

The cosmos mandate that you sail away,
Yet grotesque insects block your path.
You stop, unwilling to face their wrath.
I catch up, a heart filled with false hope.
Yet though a broken pattern has delayed you,
And allowed my chain and I to find you,

We still were never meant to know each other.
You belong to worlds beyond my reach;
And so we split across the ageing bridge
I go forward into a watery gate.
You go left into another realm.

Question 1

⊙

Please could share with us your experience regarding this poem and what inspired you to write it?

Virgil: I wrote that poem a while ago during a visit to the city of Pittsburgh. One of the neat features of Pittsburgh is that there are three rivers flowing through it. This makes it a very interesting city from a magical perspective because the energetic dynamics underlying the area are quite unique. Each of the rivers is inhabited by a river deity, and since I used to visit the city often, I got to know each of them well.

The poem is about a time I was walking to the Monongahela River in order to converse with its river deity. There is a highway on a bridge. If you walk along the sidewalk, you come to a very high staircase near Duquesne University. I was walking down the staircase. There was a woman in front of me also walking down it. She was very pretty and was talking on her phone. Based on what I heard from her side of the conversation, she seemed really interesting. In addition, her voice was just so bubbly and cheerful, so it stuck out to me since I had purposely built up a solemn and reserved mood within myself in order to more easily enter the state of trance I needed to be in to talk to the river deity. I was still somewhat afraid of heights at the time, so I walked down the stairs slowly. She was practically jogging down them and wasn't afraid at all. At the bottom, she reached a street and waited for traffic to stop so she could cross to the other side. From my perspective, since I was so high up, the cars looked like beetles. Anyhow, the traffic took a while to stop, and by the time it did, I had actually caught up with her again. She had ended her phone conversation by this point. I wanted to talk to her, since she seemed really interesting, but I also didn't want to creep her out so I didn't. Anyhow, when the traffic finally stopped, we walked across the street onto another bridge which was painted yellow. Upon reaching the other side, she turned left and I went forward to look for another staircase that led down to the riverbank.

Question 2

☉

Could you share with us your background regarding your journey along the esoteric path?

Virgil: Most people's paths are messy and unfocused at the very beginning. Mine was like that too. When it came to occultism and magic, I was interested in everything – Ceremonial Magic, Evocation, Huna, Reiki, Kabbalah, Shamanism, Runes, Tarot, Hoodoo, Wicca, etc. I read every book I had access to. I tried every exercise and practice I could find. I suppose a description of this period of my life might be interesting to some people, but not in any meaningful way. In retrospect, I was wasting my time. There's a well-known saying " –The hunter who chases two rabbits catches neither one." I wasn't chasing two rabbits. I was chasing around fifty or sixty rabbits. Whether or not a person manages to clean up his magical life and get it focused is pretty much what determines whether or not he makes any real progress. There were some incidents along the way that helped me do this.

For example, I used to live near one of the ten best research libraries in the United States. When I moved to that location, one of the first things I did was visit it. Since I was interested in Buddhism, I went to the Buddhism section. It was enormous and filled with a number of extremely rare Buddhist texts. I remember thinking to myself "Wow, how am I going to read all of these in one lifetime?" Later on that night, I was thinking about this and I realized maybe it wasn't such a good idea to try to do that. Instead, I went online and found a copy of the Dhammapada. Instead of trying to read through fifty or more rare Buddhist texts, I ended up reading and rereading the Dhammapada over and over again, studying it carefully. That was a lot more beneficial for me. I only went back to the Buddhist section of that library maybe two or three times before moving away from the area.

Of course, learning about IIH was the single most important event that helped me to organize and focus my path. It was a major transitional point for me. I had to learn new things, obviously, but I also had to unlearn a lot of stuff. I sold many of the books I owned. That took a while, almost a year to do. I didn't own a personal computer back then, but I guess the modern equivalent would be removing bookmarks and deleting PDFs. After that, it was just a matter of patiently and persistently completing the exercises in the order Bardon arranged them.

Question 3

⊙

When did you begin working through Bardon's system, and what inspired you to do so?

Virgil: For several reasons, I'd rather not say exactly when I began working through IIH. One of the reasons is this. Some people think that just because someone has been working through IIH for a long time, they must be an adept and therefore everything they say is the word of an incarnate deity. That is false. Other people think that just because someone has only been working through IIH for a very short time, they must have nothing useful to say and are not worth listening to. That is equally false. I don't want the way my writings are received to be influenced by how long I have been training in the Bardon system and applying the skills I have developed.

As for what inspired me to begin working through Bardon's system, I would say my love for the four elements, especially air, and the fact that Bardon's emphasis on direct work with the elements via pore breathing allows you to build up a much more intimate relationship with them than other systems can provide you with. Working with the elementals in PME is also a part of that too. These days, I converse with Capisi all the time. Sometimes I wonder if I should have chosen a major that would have led me down a career path in which I could work to reduce air pollution. It's too late for that, but my current career does allow me to work to improve society and the environment in a different but equally important way. My magical training, of course, is centered around shaping myself so that I can do this as well as possible.

Question 4

⊙

What are the differences are between someone working through IIH and someone working with other magical systems?

Is it possible to obtain the same results in both?

Virgil: This is an interesting and very important question. I partially address it at various points in my new book. Here I will try to give a concise answer. In the introduction to his book. *How To Speak To Saturn*, Bill (William Mistele) writes:

> *The purpose of this book is straightforward and simple. It is my intent to place into the hands of people a means to eliminate corruption in government and to free the world of war and also of dictators.*

When Chaos magicians, Thelemites, or Golden Dawn magicians write books, do you see them making statements like that in the introduction?

To put it bluntly, Bardon's system is completely different from Chaos Magic, Thelema, and the Golden Dawn system. The modern adept Frater Acher wrote a very well-known essay called, *On Power and Magic*. In it, he divides a magical system into three aspects, which he calls the "What Circle", the "How Circle", and the "Why Circle". These three circles are like layers of an onion. The What Circle is the surface layer of the system. The Why Circle is the heart of the system. Bardon's system might overlap a little with other systems on the level of the What Circle and maybe even the How Circle, but its Why Circle is drastically different from the Why Circles of other systems and traditions of magic. Therefore, despite surface similarities it might have with them, the Bardon system is fundamentally and essentially different from those other systems and traditions of magic.

Or, to put it another way, and answer one of your questions, yes, they do serve different purposes. Chaos Magic has never been clearly defined, so

I will not try to comment on it. Crowley's system is designed to help people find their "true will". Bardon did not believe in a true will. The idea behind a true will, according to Crowley, is that there is one ideal path in life that a person should follow to maximize his happiness and fulfillment in life. This idea reflects a simplistic view of the universe. In IIH, Bardon has you working with akasha a lot. Akasha is a substance which gives rise to not just infinite possibilities, but also infinite actualities. It transcends both space and time. It is omnipotent. It is the source of anything and everything. The more you work with akasha, the more you learn to view things from the perspective of akasha. Once you do this, the idea that there is only one single pre-set path for everyone to follow ends up seeming kind of silly. There are good things about Crowley's system, and many of his writings are useful, but Crowley's system and Bardon's system are essentially different and were created for different purposes.

When a Bardonist completes IIH and begins learning and working with the spirits of PME, he will find there are many possible ways he can use the skills he developed during his basic training and numerous spirits to assist him with whatever he decides to do. What he does with his abilities and what spirits he chooses to work with and learn from is all up to him. These choices are his to make and are not predetermined by some "true will" he has to adhere to. The possibilities and opportunities open to him are infinite and endless.

It is a similar situation with the Golden Dawn system. The purpose of the Golden Dawn system, according to its Adeptus Minor ritual, is to,

> *....apply myself to the Great Work, which is to purify and exalt my Spiritual Nature so that with the Divine Aid I may at length attain to be more than human, and thus gradually raise and unite myself to my higher and Divine Genius.*

This is not the purpose of the Bardon system. In the Bardon system, it's just an exercise. It's found in Step 10 of IIH. IIH is just the beginning. It's a training manual, however, the question one must ask is what exactly are we training for? Soldiers don't train just for the sake of training. They train so they can go to war and defend their country. Firefighters don't train just for the sake of training. They train so they can extinguish fires and save lives.

Similarly, the Bardonist trains, not just for the sake of training, but so he is better able to accomplish a task. Finding what exactly that task is will lead one to discover the purpose of the Bardon system. I won't go too much into detail about what that purpose is, although I will say this. A good friend of mine, another magician who has also worked through IIH, once said to me "I think people should laugh and smile more." That statement lies very close to the purpose of the Bardon system. Bardon lived during a time of great suffering. He wanted to see more joy in the world, and thus, he created a system of training to teach people how to fill the world with joy. In Kabbalah, Tiphereth is the centre of the Tree of Life and transmits light/joy to all other parts of the universe. Tiphereth is also the sephirah associated with adepthood, according to Bardon in PME. On page 304, he writes,

> *As soon as the sphere magician is master of the Sun sphere, there exists no problem anymore which he would not be able to solve in the right way. His knowledge has no gap and by means of this sphere, he is able to become a perfect adept.*

For Bardon, an adept is like the sun because he is a master of the art of filling the world with joy and light.

So, to summarize, the purpose of Crowley's system is to help people find their "true will." The purpose of the Golden Dawn system is to help people exalt their spirits in order to connect with something more divine than their mundane egos. The purpose of the Bardon system is to help people become co-creators of the universe so they can recreate the world into one filled with joy and light. Those interested in practical esoteric work need to first determine what they want to get out of their studies and then choose the system that will help them accomplish their goals. For me, that is the Bardon system, and there has never been a conflict between my own reasons for training in magic and the inner inspiration and purpose at the heart of that system. They align perfectly, and that is how I know the Bardon system, as opposed to Thelema or the Golden Dawn system, is the right system for me.

Question 5

⊙

How do you feel about ritual magic, and what relation does it have to IIH?

Virgil: I spent a few years practising ritual and ceremonial magic. That was a long time ago. It never really resonated well with me, so I abandoned those practices. How you practically apply the skills you develop during your training process is really a matter of personal preference. IIH is basic training. Whatever ritual magic is, it can hardly be said to fall into the category of basic training. A lot of people don't realize that, and this is where the problems begin. For example, in the Golden Dawn system, the dagger is the ritual tool that corresponds with the Air Element. It represents, among other things, a sharp mind. Therefore, whenever you hold an air dagger, you are asserting that you have a sharp mind. But if you don't actually have a sharp mind, then you are lying.

The fire wand represents a strong will. Whenever you hold a fire wand, you are asserting that you have a strong will. But again, if you don't actually have a strong will, you are lying.

Whenever you stand in the centre of a ritual circle, you are asserting that you are connected with Divinity. However, if you have not actually connected with Divinity by entering an akashic trance and elevating your consciousness, then once again, you are lying.

Magic centres around truth. Levi says that the woman in the last Tarot card, The Universe, embodies Absolute Truth. Bardon says that only someone who seeks the truth is suitable to begin magical training. Ironically, a lot of "magical" rituals are nothing more than a series of lies. When you pick up your air dagger, you are lying. When you pick up your fire wand, you are lying. When you stand in the centre of your ritual circle, you are lying. The thing is, just because a ritual is just one lie after another doesn't mean it won't work. Such a magical ritual still might bring you some fast cash or a date with a hot girl. However, in the

Bardon system, magic is not about nudging the astral light every now and then in order to increase your material pleasures. It's about embodying the highest forms of power and wisdom in order to accomplish divine missions that make human society more blessed and increase the amount of joy in the world.

Therefore, from a genuine magician's point of view, a student of magic should remain focused on his basic training. For the Bardonist, that consists of the work found in IIH.

Question 6

⊙

Many students of Bardon's system have problems with VOM in Step I. Why is this the case?

Virgil: I think it's hilarious. VOM is by far the easiest and most straightforward exercise in IIH. Of course, that is only the case if you first become proficient in the first mental exercise, which is thought-observation. Otherwise, VOM is impossible. Thought-observation is actually my favorite exercise in IIH. It is also the foundation of the entire mental aspect of magical training. Because of its importance, I devote an entire chapter to just that one exercise in my new book.

Question 7

⊙

You state that thought-observation is your favourite exercise and that those who underestimate its importance do so to their own detriment. Despite this, the first chapter of your book (The Spirit of Magic) is the one about asana, not thought observation. Why is this?

Virgil: There are several reasons for this. The main reason is that the asana chapter is not just a commentary on the specific practice of asana. It also serves to introduce some important generic ideas about magical training in general.

In addition, gaining a basic mastery over your body, which is the purpose of asana, is equally as important as gaining a basic familiarity with your mind, which is the importance of thought-observation. Therefore, asana is an essential exercise, but compared to other essential exercises like visualization and meditation, it is not as widely practiced or discussed in magical circles. I guess putting the asana chapter first was kind of my way of saying to people "Hey, this exercise is important too!"

Question 8

⊙

Over the years, you must have had many conversations with people interested in esotericism and magic. When it comes to these conversations, what is your biggest pet peeve?

Virgil: My biggest pet peeve would be coming across people disparaging, belittling, or condemning a specific religion, religion in general, or religious people. I have no tolerance for that.

Question 9

⊙

Could you explain what the most inspirational teachings you have discovered are and why you find them to be inspirational?

Virgil: The most inspirational teachings I have come across are those woven into William Mistele's writings. If you read one of his evocation accounts or essays about, say, Cigila, you can't help but reflect upon the fact that contained within the essay is a small portion of the wisdom and knowledge of a powerful being who is connected with Divinity and guides the evolution of the human race. It is incredible when you think about it.

I guess the main reason why I find Bill (William Mistele) so inspiring is that he writes what he knows to be true, regardless of how much it clashes with traditional or standard beliefs and dogma. He knows that the stuff he writes is true because it is based on his own personal experience. For example, in many of his essays, he claims that you can practice evocation without a wand, circle, triangle, altar, or any other tools or paraphernalia. To make a claim like that, you either need a lot of balls or complete indifference to whatever the current established ideology of the occult world happens to be.

Most traditional magicians would dismiss Bill's claim as nonsense, but it is true, and he knows it to be true because it is based on his own evocations. When Bill evokes a spirit, he just sits in a chair, uses Step 5 techniques to fill the atmosphere around him with the appropriate element or light-fluid, and then invites the spirit into the room. There's no circle, wand, triangle, sword, or censer involved at all.

Question 10

⊙

The plot of your short story titled "A Modern Fairy Tale" involves a magician who tries to perform astounding magical feats in public but then finds that he has suddenly lost all of his magical abilities. Why would this happen?

Virgil: The reason is that if you do something like that, you are going to seriously disrupt a lot of people's spiritual evolution. Divine Providence is not going to approve of this and will stop you. The first step in advancing spiritually is to learn to have faith. This is true for any spiritual path. If you definitively prove to someone the existence of higher powers by performing amazing magical acts, then you prevent them from learning to have faith. This would prevent them from taking the first step of spiritual evolution until their next incarnation when they no longer remember the amazing magical act. Only then do they once again have the potential to learn to have faith. At our current point in time, that's the way things are. In the far past, pretty much everyone had faith in higher powers. That's why people like the prophets could openly demonstrate incredible magical feats. In the far future, Bardon says that science will merge with magic. At that point in time, it will probably be ok to demonstrate incredible magical feats in public, after all, that is basically what technology will be. However, we do not live in the far past or the far future. We live in the present, and as such, we need to take into account the present spiritual state of humanity when we think about openly demonstrating drastic magical acts.

Question 11

⊙

Based on your experience, what do you feel is the biggest trap for those following the magical path and what can students do to avoid falling into it?

Virgil: The biggest trap is to underestimate the importance of character transformation. Of course, there is the simple fact that unless one has established an elemental equilibrium, one cannot safely practice the exercises past Step 2. However, that's not really what I'm referring to. Character transformation should not be seen as something you are doing just because you have to do it in order to move on to the later steps in IIH. The vast majority of the benefit, spiritual and material, that you derive from your magical training will come from your efforts in transforming your character. I used to be very irritable. My quality of life was very poor because of this. I lost friends. I had trouble making new friends. Few people wanted to be around me. My irritability plagued me for many years. Even if I charged and activated an electromagnetic volt programmed to bring me money and got a thousand dollars as a result, this would not make up for the poor quality of life I lived because of my irritability. My disorganization, my cluelessness, and my anti-social personality also caused me to lead a much poorer quality of life than if I did not possess those traits. When I changed them using autosuggestion, conscious eating, conscious breathing, and the magic of water, my life improved drastically. So avoid becoming attached to the idea that your life will improve if you learn to direct the elements with your wand, charge talismans, construct electromagnetic volts, create servitors, or perform rituals. The biggest thing you can do to improve your life is to change your character in a wise manner. Failing to realize this is the biggest trap a magician can fall into. In order to avoid this trap, be serious when you make your black soul mirror. Do a thorough job. Don't rush through it just to get it done. Throughout the process of discovering your negative traits via introspection, you will also discover the various ways they negatively impact your life. This will help you realize the necessity and importance of character transformation. Then, when you actually begin to transform your character, since Bardon's techniques are remarkably effective, you will begin to see immense positive changes in your life almost immediately. This will definitively prove to you that character transformation has enormous benefits.

Question 12

⊙

In your book, you defined a "valid" system of magic as a complete and balanced system. Could you explain what it means for a system to be complete and balanced?

Virgil: A complete system is one that contains all the exercises and practices you need in order to advance safely. Some people think that just because a system is very complicated, full of teachings, and filled with exercises, it is complete. This is not true. A system could have a million exercises and practices but still be missing the few basic essential ones. In that case, it still would not be complete. All in all, completeness is not a difficult concept to understand. Balance is slightly more difficult to understand. There are two types of balances a system should have. The first is a balance between the four elements. The second is a balance between the three planes. Any advanced student of magic can create a basic training system that is complete and has a balance between the four elements. However, only a true adept can create a system that is also balanced between the three planes because this requires a much deeper understanding of the subtle bodies and inner worlds to do. Therefore, in IIH, it is in the balance and explicit differentiation between the physical, astral, and mental aspects of training that Bardon's genius really shows itself. How complete and balanced a system is will determine how far along the road of magical advancement it can take you. In IIH, Bardon says his system is designed to guide students to "the deepest initiation and the highest wisdom." Therefore, he did his utmost best to make his system as complete and balanced as possible. For this reason, I use IIH repeatedly throughout my book to demonstrate and illustrate the concepts of completeness and balance.

Question 13

⊙

A lot of people want to lead easy and pleasurable lives. In order to do this, they cast spells whenever they encounter a problem in order to make the problem go away, and they cast spells whenever they want something in order to get it. What do you think of this?

Virgil: That kind of attitude and approach to life is very far removed from anything that could possibly fall under the category of genuine magic. Magic is closely tied to wisdom. Wisdom is closely tied to understanding. Therefore, magic is closely tied to understanding. In her book *A Wizard of Earthsea*, Ursula Le Guin writes about how magic must be worked in harmony with "the Balance and the Pattern" in order to avoid catastrophic results. Life is filled with uncertainty, so it is always a wise choice to actively prepare for any problems that may come your way in the future. Some people build up a giant collection of spells and rituals gathered together from various books, websites, modern grimoires, courses, articles, and blogs, thinking that is the best way to prepare for any problem they may encounter in life. This is a naïve solution. These people do this do not understand the Balance and the Pattern of life:

- They do not understand the Balance and the Pattern of society.
- They do not understand the Balance and the Pattern of their fates.
- They do not understand the Balance and the Pattern of spiritual evolution.

Fortunately, they almost always lack the power needed to do any major or lasting damage to the Balance and the Pattern of these things when they carry out their magical workings. In PME, Bardon says that a true magician is a master of his fate. To become a master of one's fate implies that the magician understands his fate.

In other words, he is able to see and understand the Balance and the Pattern of his fate. Once he has reached this level, he is able to directly modify that Balance and Pattern in a wise manner. This is powerful magic, but in order to perceive and work with the Balance and the Pattern of his fate, a magician needs to be proficient in working with akasha.

Immature people are unable to access akasha, and only immature people would think that the best way to deal with life is to cast spells to make all their problems go away and get whatever they want. From a magician's point of view, the best way for a beginning student of magic to prepare for all the potential problems in life is to transform himself so that he possesses all of the qualities (organization, intelligence, astuteness, etc.) needed to successfully deal with most major issues. This can be done via the techniques of autosuggestion, conscious eating, conscious breathing, and the magic of water.

My words should not be interpreted to mean that practical magic should never be used to improve one's life. However, the student should first strive to develop the wisdom needed to discern when practical magic will actually help him and when it will only mess up his life further because of the way the magic is carried out. Again, wisdom and understanding are closely tied to each other, so to develop wisdom, one should develop an understanding of oneself. The soul mirrors are a great way of doing this. As can be seen, in the beginning of IIH, Bardon is already preparing the student so that by the time he learns to work practical magic with the fluid condensers and the elements in later steps, he will be able to carry out that work wisely and responsibly. This has nothing to do with morals or ethics.

If you want to use magic to make your life easy and pleasurable, there is absolutely nothing wrong with that. However, just make sure you are actually making your life easy and pleasurable, and not doing the exact opposite because you are approaching your magical work in an ignorant manner. The inner dynamics underlying a person's current situation, their relation to the person's fate, and the way they are tied to the Balance and Pattern of his life can be quite complex at times. To fully understand these things and work with them requires genuine magical training, and not just gathering a bunch of spells and rituals to use when problems or obstacles pop up.

Question 14

⊙

In your last blog post in "Emerald Force," you spoke about differentiating between "magicians" and "occultists". I wonder if you could please expand on this for us, including a definition for each category.

Virgil: A magician is someone who practices magic. An occultist is someone who practices occultism. As for the difference between magic and occultism, instead of explaining it directly, I think it is better to do so using analogies. Magic is a pie. Occultism is a pie crust. Magic is a living human being. Occultism is a corpse. Magic is a Taylor Swift concert. Occultism is a video of a Taylor Swift concert uploaded to YouTube. Magic is gold. Occultism is iron pyrite.

Question 15

⊙

Can you briefly discuss the nature of Bardon's third book The Key to the True Quabbalah (KTQ)? How does the "Quabbalah" Bardon teaches in his book relate to or differ from traditional (Jewish) Kabbalah?

Virgil: Bardon couldn't have cared less about traditional Kabbalah. His third book is about the art of creative speaking. Therefore, its title really should have been The Key to Creative Speaking. He chose to refer to the art of creative speaking as "Quabbalah" for advertising purposes because Kabbalah was a subject of much interest in the esoteric community back then, as it is now. While the art of creative speaking, is in fact, a part of traditional Kabbalah (as shown by passages in the Sepher Yetzirah referencing this art), it is hardly unique to that spiritual tradition. It was also practised by adepts belonging to a diverse array of spiritual traditions from Egypt, India, and many other places in the world. In his third book, Bardon teaches the art of creative speaking in its most pure form, stripped of all the various cultural add-ons and adornments various mystical and magical traditions have slapped onto the art. Bardon learned the art of creative speaking in its original pure form from the Earthzone spirit Amalomi. This Earthzone spirit, like all the other Earthzone spirits listed in PME, does not belong to any specific spiritual tradition, and neither does the art she teaches.

QUESTION 16

⊙

FROM THE WISDOM THAT YOU HAVE RECEIVED NOW, WHAT ADVICE WOULD YOU OFFER TO THE YOUNGER ASPECT OF YOURSELF IF THE TWO OF YOU WERE TO MEET?

Virgil: Some people say there are three kinds of people – those who make things happen, those who watch things happen, and those who have no idea what the hell is happening. I would tell my younger self not to be the type of person who has no idea what the hell is happening. I think that's a large part of what the first power of the sphinx, "To Know," is all about. It's not about memorizing tables of correspondences or studying occult philosophy. It's about being aware of your situation and environment, as well as understanding what is going on within you and around you. This is something that will benefit all aspects of your life, not just the aspects relating to magic. Those who are familiar with the Harry Potter series might recognize Severus Snape as an illustration of the importance of truly understanding your situation. He didn't quite get why Lily was drifting away from him until it was too late. Then, when she was dead, he learned to embody the first power out of necessity. He was at Dumbledore's right hand as well as Voldemort's. He knew perfectly well what was happening. And that's not all. He also made things happen. He was not just a wizard; he was a magician.

Question 17

⊙

Many people these days claim to be adepts, but of course, only a small fraction of these people have really reached that level. What is the best way to determine an individual's true level of magical advancement?

Virgil: Examine his writings or other works, in particular, those that are intended to be critical in nature. Look to see if the language he uses is unnecessarily hurtful. Of course, there is nothing wrong with criticism, and a mature person will always welcome constructive criticism. However, criticism that is worded in an unnecessarily hurtful or insulting way is a glaring sign that the giver of criticism cannot be past Step 2 or the equivalent level of whatever training system he is using, assuming the system in question is complete and balanced. Otherwise, it is not worth considering. I have come across people who have attained adept-level ranks in some training systems yet they are still just plain mean, rude, and even petty at times. It's sad that there are people like this, but a recognition of the fundamental attainments of an initiate that are universal across all training systems (like establishing an elemental equilibrium) will be useful in differentiating between those who are adepts by meaningful standards and those who are adepts by modern standards.

QUESTION 18

⊙

COULD YOU COULD TELL US A BIT MORE ABOUT YOUR BOOK THE SPIRIT OF MAGIC: REDISCOVERING THE HEART OF OUR SACRED ART[17]. WHAT WAS THE INSPIRATION BEHIND IT, AND WHAT CAN WE EXPECT TO FIND IN IT?

Virgil: Writing the book was an act of love. For me, to love someone is to work to ensure he or she experiences as much joy and fulfillment in life as possible. I think serious magical training will help people become successful, achieve their greatest potential, and get the most out of their lives. For this reason, I wrote the book. Its main purpose is to help students train efficiently and effectively, as well as to help them avoid common pitfalls.

The original source of inspiration for the book is the most beautiful woman I ever met. I have no idea where she is now, but sometimes when I close my eyes, I can still see her wearing a brilliant blue shirt with her name on the back while sitting on a chair in a reading room filled with sunlight streaming in through glass walls. I feel a strange sense of contentment when that happens as if I am being reminded of some divine principle that is beyond words but flows through the very heart of magic. The image is just as vivid as my actual experience the day I first ran across her. A lot of occultists talk about undergoing intense mystical experiences and spiritual transformations when meditating. Maybe that actually happens, and maybe it doesn't. But when you meet a beautiful woman who embodies harmony, peace, compassion, freedom, intelligence, and the ecstasies of the four elements, and then converses with her for even a few seconds, that is genuinely a mystical and transforming experience. In fact, sometimes, such an experience can be so intense that its effects on you eventually compel you to write a five hundred page book in order to even begin processing what the heck happened to you."

---

[17] https://amzn.to/3l3kIA0

Question 19

☉

Can you elaborate some more on the meaning of your book's subtitle, Rediscovering the Heart of Our Sacred Art? What is the heart of magic, and how did it become so lost that we must work to rediscover it?

Virgil: In IIH, Bardon states that Jesus was one of the greatest magicians who ever lived. Such a statement has many important implications, but unfortunately, most people don't understand it. They think that Bardon said this because Jesus could walk on water, turn water into wine, and levitate. That's hardly the reason Bardon considered Jesus a great magician. In the well-known Christmas carol Hark the Herald Angels Sing, there is a line that goes as follows " –Light and life to all he brings, ris'n with healing in his wings." That's why Bardon considered Jesus to be a great magician. All his life, Jesus worked to bring light and life to everyone around him. He raised himself up spiritually so he could heal others. Within that line is the heart of magic.

As for how the heart of magic was lost, that's a more difficult question to answer because there were a number of factors involved in the process. As you are probably aware, Kabbalah in its original form was far more magical than mystical. Someone analyzing texts like the Sepher Yetzirah and the Zohar through the eyes of an initiate can see this very easily. In traditional Kabbalah, humility was said to be the most important quality a student could possess. When I first learned this, I thought it was weird. I could see why it was important, but I couldn't see why it was considered the most important and held in high esteem above all other virtues and positive traits. I believe I see why now, and I bring this up because I think it is relevant to your question. Magical lore states that the magicians of Atlantis were very powerful, but they used their power unwisely. This lead to the destruction of the continent, and the near-destruction of the human race. The root cause of that catastrophe was the arrogance of the magicians. They thought they could force the currents of the inner planes to act against the harmony of nature and the will of Divine Providence.

In more modern times, if you examine the bickering and feuding that has plagued occult schools and groups in the past century or so, a lot of it also arises from arrogance. When magicians allowed themselves to become arrogant, they began to lose sight of the heart of their sacred art. In modern times, whenever you come across a self-proclaimed adept, magician, or magical authority, examine his words, writings, and other works to see if you can detect any trace of arrogance in his personality. This will help you assess his actual level of magical advancement."

Question 20

⊙

Is there anything else you would like to add?

Virgil: I'll leave you with a proverb my friend Kayley is very fond of –

"Condemnation without investigation is the height of ignorance."

CHAPTER 10: WILLIAM R. MISTELE

INTRODUCTION

I was born in Detroit, Michigan. My parents were extraordinarily dynamic. They were patrons of all the major Christian evangelists in the United States. They had contact with many political and business leaders. When it came to motorboats, sailboats, planes, and cars, they either set new records or owned some of the most famous ones in the world.

In this enchanting environment, you could come down to breakfast in the morning and meet a house guest like Captain Fuchida who led the Japanese attack on Pearl Harbor. You could hear the Captain and my mother discussing previously undisclosed details about the causes of World War II.

However, surrounded as I was by relatives who were masters of engineering, business enterprise, law, and accounting, I pursued a different path.

I graduated from Wheaton College in Wheaton, Illinois with a BA in philosophy and a minor in economics. At that time, I began studying esoteric, oral traditions. In genuine mythology, individuals come into contact with the creative powers of the human spirit. Words and language possess a symbolic and imaginative quality that is magical. To understand an idea is to experience it from within. This involves a life-long, transforming journey if you change the self, you change the world.

As part of my field research, I lived in a Tibetan Buddhist monastery in Berkeley, California. I next studied Hopi Indian culture and language at the University of Arizona where I received a Masters degree in linguistics. At that time I became the only accepted student of a Hopi Indian shaman.

While living in Tucson, Arizona I began studying the Western hermetic traditions and the nature religions of Wiccans and Druids. I worked with a number of extremely gifted psychics and parapsychologists whose primary focus was on experimentation and research. I also practiced evocation with a Sufi master.

I then moved to Hawaii in 1982. There I studied with the relocated abbot of a Taoist monastery that existed for over two thousand years in China, a Vietnamese Zen master, and one of the foremost Tai Chi Chuan masters of China.

Since 1975, I have been a steadfast student of the system of initiation taught by the Czech magician, Franz Bardon, who died in the fifties. This system has provided the methods for contacting nature spirits and interacting with them in a personal and original manner. Franz Bardon's mission was to offer a system of self-initiation that maximizes the spiritual powers and creativity of the individual.

Over the years I have worked as a group facilitator and a mediator in family and divorce mediation. I have taught as a civilian instructor for the U.S. Navy and marines. I have researched investing strategies for individuals' portfolios. I am also a lifelong student researching strategies for resolving international conflicts.

I consider myself a spiritual anthropologist. Expanding on Bardon's purposes, I am integrating into his system the wisdom of all traditions. To this end, I have created a new genre of modern fairy tales. These stories are not about belief or faith but direct experience. They open gates to other realms where we discover the keys to what is missing from life.

In 1998, I created a teaching website where I post my research and writings. This site currently offers a free correspondence course and ongoing seminar for developing undine empathy. I am also establishing an archive on this site that gathers individuals' experiences with undines from around the world. The goal is to expand and add clarity to the body of world literature in this area.

~ William R. Mistele

Questions & Answers

Question 1

⊙

Could you please tell us a little about your journey? How did you come to find Bardon's works and what inspired you to follow this path?

William: My life path was dramatically shaped by nightmares beginning when I was around seven years old. I would sit in a fundamentalist Christian church and the preachers would preach about hellfire. And then I went to elementary school and the teachers had us practice "duck and cover." This was a method of protecting yourself in case of a nuclear war. You hide under your desk as a three-megaton nuclear missile from Russia vaporizes the city of Detroit where I lived. There was a fire in the inner spiritual/religious world and fire in the external world, though obviously the fire in the external world was produced by human beings.

Furthermore, there is speculation that we almost lost the city of Detroit in 1966 when a breeder reactor south of the city was at risk of a reactor core meltdown. So the question dawning in my mind over the years was where is the wisdom that governs society and nations so that human beings can possess things like the nuclear fusion of the sun without destroying themselves.

And speaking for myself, this question about wisdom governing nations was part of why Franz Bardon wrote his three books. Supposedly, people, who died in World War I complained to Divine Providence that they had no genuine teacher when they were alive.

It took forty years and an even worse world war for Divine Providence to respond to these complaints through the publication of Franz Bardon's three books. Consequently, in my mind, the first thing some of Bardon's students might direct their attention to is putting an end to wars.

Eventually, a trained Bardon student is able to look into the minds of anyone on earth and evaluate their karma (or let's say their positive and negative traits) as well as the karma of nations. And this is not pretentious or overreaching. The human race since the fifties has at least six times been minutes and sometimes seconds away from an all-out nuclear exchange.

At least four of the 360 Earthzone spirits Bardon describes specialize in issues of war and peace and the fate of nations. These spirits send their vibrations and inspiration through the entire planet earth for four minutes each day. Consequently, they are already right here talking to all of us daily. You just have to listen. I do a lot of listening. So for me, it is the most natural thing in the world to want to learn from such divine spirits. I would like to act on their wisdom so that diplomats and national leaders are more skilled, wiser, and committed to benevolent outcomes in their international interactions.

This "can-do" approach I acquired from growing up in my family. I would come home from school and there was my father in the backyard grilling hamburgers for people such as the vice president of Ford Motors, the mayor of Grosse Pointe, the Chief of Police, the CEO of the largest retail store in the U.S, etc. My father was later asked to be press secretary for a presidential candidate.

My uncle oversaw General Motors operations in its manufacturing of weapons in WWII. My mother had long conversations about who started WW II with Captain Fuchida who was the pilot who led the attack on Pearl Harbor. My father organized a "reunion" of Japanese and American admirals and generals in Honolulu for the anniversary of the Pearl Harbor attack.

In my family of origin, I met people who were not just involved in world-historic events. They helped shape these events. And yet there remained this void, a terrible absence of wisdom, regarding how to communicate, understand, negotiate, and resolve conflicts between nations. The external world does not have adequate tools for solving these problems. To find what I was looking for, I needed greater wisdom and a perspective on human history and a means for transforming human nature.

In 1970, when I was out of college, I began studying spiritual anthropology. I wanted to extract methods for transforming consciousness that was drawn from the oldest esoteric traditions on earth. I wanted a psychic, magical, and spiritual set of practices. This was in part because it was clear to me that the previous five hundred years of Protestant interpretation existed in a spiritual vacuum. They emphasized the reading of words without any self-reflective, contemplative, meditative, or intuitive training of any kind. I had met a great many Christian teachers before I went to college and so I had a fairly accurate basis for my conclusions.

I then studied with many masters of a variety of traditions. In 1975, I began visualizing for half an hour each day on the first three Tarot cards–the Magician, Isis, and the Fool. I then had a dream about finding four magic books, the first three were Bardon's. Shortly after this, a friend handed me *Initiation into Hermetics,* which she thought I might be interested in. I immediately began to study this book seriously, since I had been looking for something like this for ten years previously.

Question 2

⊙

When you were working your way through IIH, which step did you feel was most difficult for you and why? In addition, how did you overcome this challenge?

William: For the first ten years, I tried to follow Bardon's instructions exactly as he offers them. I started over from the beginning at least seven times.

The problem is, I can get a lot of things to work for me the way they are taught. But at a certain point, my body and nervous system refuse to cooperate.

Take the lung and pour breathing exercise. I could do that. And I could get a sensation of emitting waves of light from the condensed vitality I had compressed within my body. Years later after interviewing "incarnated mermaids," I realized these individuals were using the water element to heal others, sometimes healing even terminal patients.

By contrast, Bardon was emphasizing a fiery kind of vitality–it is hot, condensed, dynamic, pressured, and explosive. On the other hand, the watery method of healing is gentle, soft, soothing, extremely empathic, extraordinarily clairsentient, and it operates like dialysis–it takes and purifies the individual's vitality.

My body is oriented toward the watery form of healing. Given who I am, Bardon's method was the worst kind of vitality for me to work with, in the beginning.

Equally disastrous for me was Bardon's mental exercises, involving concentration. Though concentration is natural for me when I do it as Bardon presents the exercises energy gets trapped in my third eye and I get terrible headaches. Again, my nervous system requires a different approach. Namely, by meditating on the void–as being nothing and part of a vast space of nothingness/emptiness/void–energy does not get stuck in any part of my body. There is no image or outline of my body present in those meditations so there is nowhere for the energy to get stuck or blocked.

And similarly, any ritual magic involving visualizing circles, triangles, pentagrams, or the use of magical tools like crystals, wands, robes, magic mirrors, etc. simply shorts out my nervous system and causes physical ailments. My body is so sensitive that I cannot even wear jewellery.

Over the years, another problem that I ran into with the early chapters of IIH has been with the soul mirror and magical equilibrium. Again, it is easy enough for me to follow the directions as presented. I can say to myself, "Oh. There is this fire element within me. It is in part positive and also in part negative. It makes me insatiable curious beyond what I have met in any other human being". And it gives me an immediate and nearly absolute certainty that there are solutions that can be found to solve any problem. This is Sagittarius energy with positive and negative aspects.

And this fiery sense of command and vision come from both my mother and father. Looking back, I was exposed to the cosmic letter K with its fiery sense of absolute command. And my father used that authority so well that mafia dons had respect for him, not because he was bad. Rather, he could do what they could not do–get men to work extremely hard and be completely loyal to him far beyond what the mafia was capable of doing.

But such primordial command is easily interwoven with negative traits as well. The alpha male often will use his position of power to absorb the will, the emotional life, and life force of others into himself. It has taken me forty-five years to find a meditation that would free me of that kind of negativity.

In other words, what appears as a personal vice or weakness may connect directly to a collective/archetypal conflict that exists in human civilization. In my experience, eliminating something negative like that in myself requires I go on a kind of spiritual quest and accomplish what has not been accomplished before in recorded history. To solve some problems for yourself you have to also solve the problem for all other people as well. There are times when changing oneself is simultaneously changing the world.

One day I was meditating on the void (the cosmic letter U) and the problem with my father and the cosmic letter K vanished. The void is beyond the reach of any abuse of power or anything negative. It would have saved me forty years of failed or misdirected efforts in magical training if someone, in the beginning, had said to me, "Oh. Your nervous system is not like other human beings. You need to begin meditating on the cosmic letter U. Find in yourself a stillness that embraces the universe. Then and only then through that mastery will some of these personal problems of yours disappear.

But this experience with trial and error, with experimentation with its successes and failures, served a purpose. I am a writer. I tell stories. It was essential for me to be able to trace each step between the ordinary consciousness where I began and the magical meditations I do now. I am supposed to write a manual on effective, practical, and field-tested ways for eliminating war on earth.

In the twentieth century, at least three hundred million people died of smallpox. After twelve thousand years of smallpox plagues, in 1979, through careful work, the United Nations eliminated smallpox from the earth. Eliminating war is a similar enterprise. You do the work, you get the results, *Initiation into Hermetics* is not a prayer book for the devout. You train and then you take into your hands the powers of creation.

Practising IIH is not about making little changes that upgrade your life and make you a better person. You really do not need this calibre of magical training to do something positive and constructive with your life. IIH is altogether different. It gives you the ability to act as a divine being and to interact with all aspects of human evolution.

In looking back, I think of my uncle again: when blindfolded, he could take a car engine apart and put it back together again. That is my approach to the Bardon exercises. I have to reverse engineer, experiment, modify, rewrite and compare them to what other traditions do. To take them apart and put them back together again to see how many different ways I can make them work. Then hopefully I find something that fits me personally. And in the process perhaps what I discover is useful to someone else as well.

Question 3

☉

What advice would you offer to Bardon students working their way through IIH?

William: Though IIH is self-initiation, I would recommend to you, read whatever commentaries you can find on the internet about the first book and Bardon's other books as well. Especially find questions and answers related to the chapter you are working on. Find a mentor, someone whom you can bounce ideas off of and who can assist you in solving problems.

If you have difficulties, investigate other traditions relating to the chapter you are working on. If you have trouble stopping thoughts and developing an empty mind, drop in on a Quaker, or other silence meditation group. Take a look at Zen monasteries of different national cultures, a Vipassana meditation group, or a Dzogchen Tibetan meditation group. Take a look at an Aikido dojo, a Tai Chi Chuan group, a yoga meditation group, or someone who does biofeedback, etc.

Each tradition has a slightly different perspective and understanding of how the mind works. Some first relax and energize the body through stretching which makes the mind much easier to quiet. Some do these very peaceful, hypnotic chants with incense and a restful ambience of a temple surrounding you. Spend a lot of time concentrating single-mindedly on slow movements of the body that the mind is already trained to sink "chi" downward in the body to the lower Dan Tien.

With one exercise, you may excel. With another exercise, you may need external help as if you have some sort of learning disability. Observe your progress. Discover what works for you. I could easily write an essay on Forty Things to Do with an Empty Mind. Perhaps one or two of those forty things you are already adept in. All you need to do is take what you are good at and gradually expand it so it accomplishes the purpose of the original exercise in IIH.

For me, the first three chapters in IIH are a summary of everything in Bardon's three books. Everything else is just refinement and application. The empty mind exercise turns into work on the cosmic letters E and U. The transference of consciousness exercise turns into mental wandering and contact with spirits. The astral mirror exercises turn into an understanding of others' karma and the fate of groups and nations. You take an exercise and you can explore it on multiple levels. In other words, for me, there is no end to practising the first three chapters. These first exercises just get deeper and richer.

QUESTION 4

☉

YOU HAVE GIVEN A LIST OF EXAMPLES FROM STUDENTS (IN YOUR BLOG POST)[18] WHY THEY DO NOT FULLY COMPLETE STEPS 1- 3 (IN BARDON'S IIH) OR GIVE UP. WHAT WOULD YOU SAY IN YOUR EXPERIENCE ARE THE MAIN CAUSES OF THIS?

William: For me, there is a high level of difficulty in practising IIH just because of the nature of the subject matter. Bardon has the formidable task of taking a human being and placing him on a path where he ends up reflecting the greater universe in himself. This training system is intended to give a human being the full powers of an Earthzone spirit while he is still in incarnation.

Taking on such a training system is a lot to ask of a student. It is kind of like saying, "Here is the perfection of wisdom taught systematically in ten steps that awakens you to a multi-dimensional awareness and that enables you to not only interact with beings of other realms but to make those realms a second home." You could take any chapter in IIH and use it as the central goal of an esoteric lodge, or to start a new religion.

All the same, if you pick up IIH and read the introduction, a student might imagine that with serious work he can proceed exercise by exercise and chapter by chapter and finish the book in five to ten or maybe fifteen years. And yet obviously everyone has their strengths and weaknesses that they bring to the practice.

I have sat and meditated with a Zen master. It took him fifteen years to master his first koan. He said, "it is impossible to stop your mind from thinking thoughts." That was his experience. I have sat and meditated with martial artists who have astonishing abilities in their chosen field of self-defense. Some work out for six hours every day for decades. But very few of them have any healing ability.

---

18 williammistele.com/toptenbardon3rd.htm

Similarly, I have sat in classes with world level philosophers and skilled psychologists. Again, the above individuals are genuine scholars in their chosen professions. And yet, given my interviews with various people from around the world, these philosophers and psychologists have next to no understanding of what human beings are or what they are capable of becoming. Their understanding of human nature is shaped by the ideas of a tiny intellectual community originating over here in the Western world.

When I look at what Bardon is asking the student to accomplish in chapters one through to three, he is asking for an individual who has the imagination of a Steven Spielberg. As a writer/director, give Spielberg a movie script and he has the ability to sit down and visualize all the scenes in a movie including camera angles, hear all the dialogue including sensing the feeling expressed verbally and non-verbally, and also imagine how that finished movie would play to various audiences. I think Bardon expects this level of imagination from his students.

Add to this the level of self-understanding Bardon is after in attaining astral equilibrium. It is like he wants a student to have at least the understanding that might arise from having two PhDs in psychology. After all, astrologers will talk about the traits you have from looking at your natal chart. But when has any astrologer on earth said to you, "Now I want you to master all twelve zodiac signs so that the elements of earth, air, fire, and water are equally balanced in your soul."

"If your sun sign is Leo, I want you to develop yourself so you have the open-mindedness and understanding of an Aquarian who sees the big picture in terms of what life is all about. If your sun sign is Aries and you are bold, down to earth, and assertive, I want you to equally develop the sign of Libra in yourself. Learn to produce a balance between yourself and other people. Always stay focused on the harmony of a relationship even if you have to turn into a director and producer who subtly assists another person to feel connected and happy." And so forth.

Similarly, in the Myers-Briggs Personality system, there are personality traits that are paired off together such as thinking-feeling, extrovert-introvert, judging-perceiving and so forth. But where are the psychologists who offer you a class in balancing all these opposites in yourself? Kind of like, Are you an introvert? Let's learn to be an extrovert so that feels equally comfortable.

Are you a perceiving kind of person who wants to carefully observe and draw conclusions based on direct, personal experience as opposed to an individual who wants to label things and place them in clear categories so there can be order and organization? "Well then let's learn to be organized and act as an administrator so we can get more done." Psychologists do not ask people to strive for such balance. But that is exactly what Bardon insists we accomplish.

Bardon is asking his students to balance the four elements in their souls. And yet, given the level of energies we are working with, such balance becomes essential. If you start evoking fire or water in your soul, you will need self-perception to sense how exposure to these powers of nature affect you. Astral equilibrium is not something to work at and then move on. It is a lifetime practice and some weaknesses, or negativities in the soul will require a lifetime to work out. And there is the physical level of training. And there is the physical level of training. Imagine being able to radiate vitality like the sun. Or, if you prefer, work with magnetism and watery energy to heal others. how many people do you know can heal terminally ill patients, or who can walk into an emergency room in a hospital and provide relief from pain for everyone there? I know a few individuals who can do these things. But they are not magicians or even human. They were born with those abilities which they brought with them from their own elemental realms.

All the same, Bardon is asking his students to master their own vitality as if they are sixth don Aikido master or a very gifted Tai Chi Chuan master. A lot of people just are not interested in their physical bodies to the extent Bardon demands.

For me, you can read the exercises, put in the work, and seek to move on. Or you can read the exercises and take a serious look at what Bardon is after. A magician for Bardon is a master of body, soul, and mind. He is a divine being. And such divinity in human form does not come without severe tests, difficulties, and a massive effort to overcome one's limitations.

Mastery over the physical, astral, mental, and akashic realms is a key component of Bardon's magical system. My advice is to fall in love with your body and its life force, with your soul and its feelings, and with your mind with its thinking and concentration. Each level of awareness opens up wondrous realms to be endlessly explored. Make the effort to solve your problems and in the end, it is like you will have experienced the equivalent of three or more lifetimes packed into one.

Question 5

⊙

LEADING FROM QUESTION 2, THERE IS A DANGER OF BECOMING DELUSIONAL IN YOUR PRACTICE AND CONVINCING YOURSELF THAT YOU HAVE COMPLETED A STEP AND ARE READY TO MOVE ON WHEN IN REALITY THIS MAY NOT BE THE CASE. HOW CAN THE STUDENT PREVENT THIS FROM THIS OCCURRING?

William: It might help to make the exercises a part of yourself so you live and breathe them. They are not chores or prerequisites for something that comes later. They are something you fall in love with and cherish. The feminine is nurturing, supportive, sensitive, tender, and uniting. The masculine is constantly testing, experimenting, rigorous in training demanding excellence and perfection. Both approaches are required in order to take an exercise and bring it to life within yourself.

The problem in working alone is similar to problems in any kind of self-education. I taught myself trigonometry and geometry during the summer before my senior year in high school. I was gifted in math so I managed to accomplish that without sitting in a classroom. I taught myself theology in college to validate required classes, since I felt the classroom presentations on this topic were terribly boring. Self-education in this instance was of great benefit for me because I could focus on making original observations that operated outside of traditional interpretations. In college, I also taught myself geology and validated a test, so I did not need to take any science requirements. I was not so good at this since geology requires some hands-on experience observing minerals.

When I studied Aikido I was already practicing Bardon visualization. This gave me a tremendous advantage. I could mentally rehearse various movements in my mind and so walk into class having memorized the previous session. And early on I could do things the Aikido sensei could not do if it involved concentration. But this accelerated mode of learning came with a price. My body was not used to the levels of concentration I was using and so I developed severe abdominal cramps. This would not have occurred if I had learned more slowly like other students.

I also had this idea that I could learn languages on my own since I could do very well in a classroom. But it turned out my brain would simply forget anything I had learned if I took a two-week break from studying.

It took me three years to figure out that I had a learning disability when it comes to languages. Learning a language is not like studying other things on one's own. It did not follow similar patterns and for me, it requires first-hand interaction with other people.

So a high level of self-reflection is required when teaching yourself anything. It helps to check your progress against what others are doing. It helps to keep a journal of your practices and notice where you are advancing and where you are having difficulties. Early on in my Bardon practice, I acquired a very high-level skill in clairsentience. I could feel the auras of people and of any kind of spirit anywhere. But I had to develop my own system of interpretation of what different aura vibrations meant without any assistance from others. This required rigorous observations and note-taking. But it also meant I could study the mind of masters and the qualities of spiritual beings. And I could "feel" the vibration of Bardon exercises. This meant I could "magically enhance" any meditation or exercise I did.

Sometimes this gave me a great advantage because I could sense exactly when I was doing something right. And other times magically enhanced meditations are no advantage at all. You just have to repeat the exercise over and over and observe everything you can in order to succeed.

For me, Bardon's approach goes like this: If you do not get an exercise after repeating it thirty or forty times then don't stop. Try repeating it three or four hundred times. But do not be stupid. Vary your approach and add to your practice anything you can that might assist you in mastering something.

To summarize, to overcome problems inherent in self-education you have to devise different ways of testing yourself. I went and meditated with a great many teachers so I acquired a sense of what they can and what they cannot do. And gradually I discovered my path of training.

For me, learning magic is not like learning trigonometry or German. It is more like art or storytelling. You learn the basic structure of what makes a good story. But then you have to add your own content. It takes a lot of work. But without the inspiration, you are dead in the water. You can judge for yourself if there is any value in my approach by reading my books, *Stories of Magic and Enchantment* [19]and also *Mermaid Tales*[20].

Question 6

How does one strike a balance between moving on and lingering on a step too long in an attempt to try to perfect its exercises?

William: I often get emails from students who say they have spent years and are still not through the first step. Perhaps if we had the equivalent of a magical university online, we could hold seminars and roundtable discussions about each chapter. You could ask different experienced individuals about their various approaches and suggestions.

And if we had extensive archives a beginning student could read through ten or twenty answers to a question about various difficulties and remedies for each exercise. It may be a system of self-initiation but that does not mean you should avoid learning from others or working in a group.

---

[19]https://amzn.to/3sRIJfD

[20]https://amzn.to/3gF6QsK

I would suggest a student engaged in a serious study of Western magic and the history of magic around the world. Before you study for a PhD you review the history of your field of research. It is important to be able to think critically. Answer for yourself questions such as:

— What is Bardon striving for in the mental, astral, and physical level exercises of IIH? How does IIH relate to his next two books?
— What problems crop up that prevent students from getting through the exercises at various levels?
— Who has succeeded in overcoming what appeared initially to be an insurmountable difficulty?
— Who has encountered difficulties unique to their own karma, life situation, and a set of personal aptitudes?
— What do you do when you have a PhD level of mastery of one exercise but are back in kindergarten with another exercise in the same chapter?

If you have an overview of what is being asked of you, then you can set up your own schedule and design your own personal approach to working through the exercises. Part of my training as a spiritual anthropologist is discerning the difference between what someone says they are doing and what they actually do.

If you are practicing an exercise and not getting the results you would like, then you might reexamine the way you are reading the exercise. You can ask yourself, Is there another approach I might use that would work better for me?

And this is pretty much then your question–Should I go on or spend more time deepening an exercise I feel I have already worked through? Should I pursue one exercise at a time or work at two or more exercises that seem to complement each other? The best I can suggest is that you have to experiment and observe what works for you.

If the water element were equal in strength to the fire element in society, we would have individuals who are so empathic they would be able to feel in an instant what any other person on earth is feeling. They could read others' minds, re-live others' memories, and easily see their past and their future. And they could heal terminal illnesses.

Such abilities are now present but quite rare. This means the masculine (external control of the environment, extroversion, and dynamic action, and applied force) is far more advanced in shaping human experience than is the feminine (intuitive perception, empathy, feeling, nurturing, inner soul to soul connection).

Again, the great advantage of those with strong will and power is that they know how to take charge and assume responsibility for producing concrete changes in the real world within specific time frames. With all due respect, I have not met any individuals who are deeply loving who even know what that last sentence means.
For example, for me, the evolution of government requires transparency and transparency requires that presidents and government officials do not lie and deceive. This is a red line for me. If the next president of the United States wants to govern through lies, then it is my job (using will and power) to see that those lies are quickly exposed. A just government rules through truth and this enables justice. This pursuit of justice is not a hobby of mine or something I do in my free time. I entered the world to write training manuals for accomplishing this.

Deeply loving individuals who embody the water element do not think in global, geopolitical terms. They are naturally healing. If you get near them, their aura acts to revitalize and renew your body and emotions. They spontaneously see the best in you. They act to make others feel fully alive. They are endless in their giving because they never lose their innocence. Bad experiences in the past do not shape or limit their willingness to give in the present. And often they have no ego or attachment to a social identity. They are joined from within to nature which they are a part of in the core of their being.

So how do we join the fire and water, the will and love, together? These two are not united in nature and in fact, human society has never known the primordial love in the water element. It is not present in history, in our literature, religions, or wisdom traditions.

The answer for me is that in order to apply great willpower successfully I have to always make contact with others through the extremely intuitive and empathic love that first senses and feels one with another person. When I meditate on world leaders, for example, I use an empathy that senses a oneness, as if they are me in another form. I become them in my meditation.

And then I seek to speak to them with the voice of their own conscience, the voice at the core of their being. Ideally, I present them with their own best self, their future self, a person who is completely positive, free of weaknesses, vices, and negativity.

As long as I am alive I will be involved in inspiring and guiding other individuals' lives acting as a second conscience when they have destroyed their own conscience. This is willpower but it is done through the vibration of love. My mother prayed for me every day of her life. You can say that I am carrying on her tradition of love and devotion with forty years of magical training thrown in.

However, some of the incarnated mermaid or other elemental women will often on their own join with me in meditating on various individuals just because they feel connected to me and respond to what I am interested in. Some of them are so empathic they can tell what I have been meditating on and how well that meditation is going. You could say we have a spiritual community whose members feel one with nature, one with the planet, and they seek to share that love and harmony with humanity.

Will combined with love in this sense is not the same as "I am going to produce concrete results in the real world in specific time frames." It is more like when you feel connected to the water element in nature it then becomes a part of you. Like a river that flows to the sea, your giving is inexhaustible and endless. In mystical terms, the phrase, "We are all one," is something a magician will encounter in many different ways. What we do for another we do for ourselves. Study hard and learn to do such things well. And yet the feeling of oneness is something each person must discover in their own way and through their own experience.

In every century, some individual tries to take over the world. If they have the power, they feel free to use that power almost always with terrible results. Yet for a Napoleon who seeks to be emperor, there is a George Washington who is willing to return his command to a democratic government. And there is a Churchill who refuses to surrender to a Hitler. Power can be used for good or bad.

Similarly, empathy, when free of ego and when joined to nature, has no limit set on it. You can so identify with another person that you know that person as well as he knows himself. You can act as a spirit guide, a guardian angel, a muse, a physician, a healer, a cheerleader, a life coach, and a counsellor for another person. You can literally take the roles of the ghosts of past, present, ad future as Charles Dickens described in his, "A Christmas Carol."

And then again sometimes people need to interact with the negative principle before they are willing to learn anything new. Yet when an individual so abuses his power that he harms others, then that person is acting in the public domain. The prevention of abuse and establishing justice require public oversight and the involvement of an entire community. Justice and fairness in society are everyone's responsibility. We need strong individuals of great willpower who are also so loving and empathic that even their enemies hold them in high regard and would prefer cooperating with them rather than opposing them.

I did ask the mermaid queen Isaphil one time, "When will war be no more?" Her reply was "When there shall appear on earth four or five in whom there is no fear; and whose souls are so clear that when malice, evil, or ill will draws near, these things dissolve as if they were never there.

> *When four or five shall remain in each generation, then your race shall awaken. The beauty of the stars and the seas and the mysteries shall appear within your dreams. These treasures of soul shall overflow, filling your world with light and healing.*

For me, empathy in combination with the void are the greatest power in this solar system. Will and power relate to the gathering of strength. But cosmic empathy is one with anything. Its receptivity is so great it can contain anything within itself. I hope to write a number of books, novels, and screenplays that reveal this aspect of the feminine mysteries.

In summary, the human race is fairly advanced in working with the fire, earth, and air elements. We have human beings in history who act as if they are an incarnation of the kings or queens of these three elements. But the elemental water element with its qualities of pure innocence, profound empathy, clairsentience, innate healing abilities, and intrinsic capacity to love is not well known.

You would have to increase the level of affection, love, empathy, and nurturing you find in a "normal" human man or woman by thirty times to bring the water element up to where it is equal in power to the other three elements.

Humans are way too aggressive and destructive. With thirty or forty magicians who embody the magnetic love and clairsentience of the mermaid queen, the human race can be brought back into balance. Then the magical equilibrium which we study in the first two chapters of IIH, will be more realistic and easier to attain."

Question 7

☉

Those wishing to follow a devotional/mystical path may find Bardon's approach quite clinical and scientific in the beginning since Bardon does not really address the mystical aspects until steps 9 and 10. What advice would you offer to them to aid them in progressing through Bardon's but still fulfilling that desire?

William: Yes. I agree. Bardon has no art or poetry, no songs, no spiritual/ religious services, etc. For maintaining inspiration, I would suggest that students keep a notebook of others' sayings, stories, poetry, songs, etc. that they find deeply inspirational. And then add to this any of your own insights and experiences that are inspirational. Go over these regularly. Try to produce in yourself through meditation and contemplation the original insights that inspired those who wrote these things. If others were to do this and share these experiences then you can learn from them as well. In other words, if you find anything missing in Bardon's practices, make it your personal project to fill in for what is missing and add it to the system. This then becomes your contribution.

- Do you feel there should be more discussions between students of Bardon? Set up a seminar and invite various experienced Bardon students to speak there and have round table discussions.
- Do you feel you would benefit from a spiritual/Bardon like a university? Help start such a university on the internet.
- Would you like more training videos assembled into one archive in which other students share their knowledge of how the system works? Set that up.
- Do you feel there should be a mentoring program for some of the Bardon books or art festivals, psychic readings, etc., then help with that as well? These are all contributions individuals can make. Your journey becomes part of the foundation upon which others built.

I often use the method of Eugene Gendlin called focusing. In focusing, you make direct contact with sensations and feelings within your own body relating to some question or meditation. Then you focus on this direct experience to find words or images that reflect exactly what this energy is that you are touching. The emphasis is on avoiding all labelling and moving beyond assumptions. As you work with the energy in your body this energy changes and you can then note what that change means for you. See my essay on Focusing.21

Even in the first chapter of IIH, we are describing such things as will, love, clarity of mind, and work. But those are just words. You can find common definitions for them in the dictionary but as real-life experiences, they can be profoundly different for each person.

If I am working on being mentally clear as compared to being upset, confused, or opinionated, I can recall various people and experiences in which these words apply. Some people serve as examples of clear minds and others are the opposite.

But I can also sense directly what clarity of mind is. I can focus on it. It is a feeling, a vibration, an openness, a depth of understanding, a willingness to pursue solutions without prejudice or impatience. Individuals with a clear mind do not lose their clarity no matter how

---

21 http://williammistele.com/focusing.html

much confusion or chaos is around them. With focusing, I can touch that, feel the vibration, and surround myself with it so I feel one with it.
The word clarity, love, perseverance, power, justice, etc. then become objects of meditation. They are no longer abstract. They are actual vibrations that I can study through direct experience.

Astral equilibrium itself is a meditation and contemplation. What is an individual who has balanced all four elements in himself? What is that like? How do such people operate differently? How is their conscience and intuition stronger and greater? You can work step by step toward developing the astral equilibrium in yourself. Yet in the process, you can also look ahead and imagine right now that it is completely real for you.

Bardon says to do this "imagining something is real right now." But the more imaginative, contemplative, and mystical approach is to experience this as a dream. You walk inside of it and see what differences it makes in your life. You ask questions about it and test it to see how it works. You experience the four elements in harmony with each other.

This is no small accomplishment. Because as I mention elsewhere the four elemental realms are not in harmony with each other in nature. The elemental beings do not even talk to each other. In the long term, it is up to magicians to unite the four elemental realms in their own auras and consciousness. And then to somehow communicate with other people and the world in which we live this great task of bringing all things into harmony and balance."

Question 8

☉

How do you discern true contact with the elementals versus imagined contact? Furthermore, how do we make the distinction between these two?

William: If you are asking about the difference between contacting say a real mermaid versus an imagined mermaid? A real woman, no matter how submissive, still makes demands on you. An imagined mermaid, like an imagined or fantasy woman, does not place demands on you. Men often feel that for a relationship to be real there has to be give and take– the woman has to need him in some way and he has to feel he needs her. Otherwise, there is no feeling of connection.

However, some thought-forms or created elmentaries, as well as departed spirits can have, or develop a survival instinct. In which case, they will make demands on you and want attention and energy from you.
However, as in working with a tantric image or the images of various deities and so forth, an image or symbol can be quite powerful in terms of generating feelings and new insights. I can easily take all my feelings and intuitions about the sea or a stream and shape them into an image of a woman. I can then engage this imagined woman, embodying all my conscious and subconscious connections to water in nature, in a way that makes me think new things and feel things I have not felt before.

But this kind of dialogue between my conscious mind and my subconscious mind is an art form in itself. When I write stories, I am often simultaneously taking the part of two different individuals who see and feel things from entirely different perspectives. It is a trained imagination that allows you to do this. And sometimes when I meditate, I am assuming a different form or state of consciousness that is able to act and bring about results that are far beyond what I can do in an ordinary state of mind.
You could say that during a magical action, I have temporarily created a different person who is more effective and powerful than my everyday self is. In this case, the imagined self is more real than I am at least during the magical operation.

Question 9

What exercises would you add to IIH?

William: There are some basic intellectual skills I would emphasize. I would teach beginning and advanced active listening. This enables students to listen to each other's experiences without judging and maintaining a supportive role. You will notice how some students are certain they are right or insist on their point of view. Active listening is a mindfulness practice applied to conversations. See my exercises on active *Listening and Empathy.*22

In a similar way, in the beginning, I would have students learn to articulate both sides of any position with equal enthusiasm. I learned to do this on the debating team in high school. These days it is hard to find any news anchors or new commenters who are capable of this simple level of detachment and empathy.

It helps you in discussions with others and in discovering the truth. It adds a sense of humor. And it avoids the beginner's mistake of making assumptions. In other words, take nothing for granted.

Also, learn to observe without thoughts intervening. This is the foundation of all magical training systems. In other words, use your direct perception to see or contemplate what you are observing. Thinking is best done when thoughts arise out of and are shaped by experience. This is related to having a judicial temperament. You withhold judgment until you have sufficient evidence to draw a conclusion. And you do not let ambiguity bother you.

The transference of consciousness into things and people is invaluable. This can be done extensively with animals, plants, and people as a way of knowing things from the inside. And it is great preparation for understanding spirits.

Combine the detachment of a mirror with the feeling of being one with someone. Both at once–pure detachment and simultaneously being so within someone you forget you are observing. This is itself a healing method for assisting others to attain clarity of mind and feel deeply connected to another at the same time.

Bardon says in the Epilogue to IIH,

> *It has to be taken for granted that an enormous, almost superhuman amount of endurance and patience, a tenacious willpower and secrecy regarding his progress are the fundamental conditions.*

---

22 http://williammistele.com/books.html

Or another way of saying this, to paraphrase Warren Buffett,

> *Find something in life that you love doing and then work at it with all of your heart.*

Power has its place. But for inspiration and motivation, pursue the exercises out of wonder, awe, beauty, harmony, and the way they put you in touch with the greater universe. For the powers of creation to be placed in your hands, you need to feel you are united to the unfolding of the universe. But on a practical level, I do endless interviews with people who have all sorts of siddhis beyond what general human beings possess. And every week I find myself meditating with such individuals. It is a little hard to be arrogant or delusional when I associate with others whose natural skills are far beyond what I ever imagined before meeting them.

Teachers are invaluable. But I notice that teachers are specialists. They are masters of some things but in other areas of body, history, soul, mind, or spirit, the same individual is a beginner just like anyone else and has no advantage in learning certain topics. Someone who offers a great answer to one question may be completely clueless in answering another question. You have to do your own thinking and evaluating.

In my experience, some of the Earthzone and other Spirits would teach IIH in a totally different way. A spirit who specializes in writing stories and poetry might insist you begin with writing your personal biography as a story–with an inciting incident (what got you going), a plot with subplots, acts with suspense, drama, supporting cast, opposing forces, symbols, intensifying conflict, epiphany, etc. For such a spirit, it is not possible to understand your own life much less attain any kind of astral self-understanding without knowing your own story.

Another Earthzone Spirit who specializes in symbols and communication, might insight that you begin by studying how different individuals' minds work. For such a spirit, every person sees, thinks, and feels in a different way. If you can understand others' minds, and the consciousness of animals, plants, and trees, then you are already in a position to understand most of the spirits in the universe.

The training here is just as rigorous and systematic as IIH. They just begin in a different way. If I were teaching IIH, I would begin with the five senses. I suggest in my *Five Sense Practice*, the student studies and explores each sense in terms of pleasure, bliss, ecstasy, joy, rapture, and mystery. But this is a writer's perspective. The air element on the astral plane makes an individual be artistic. It gives an acute sensitivity to the nuances of how each moment unfolds along with the suspense of not knowing what is coming next and the wonder of the unknown revealing itself as forever new.

I would also teach the void from day one. Kind of like, "Okay class. Here is your homework assignment for over the weekend. Imagine a vast, infinite space, kind of like shiny black colour with nothing in it. Now imagine this when you are interacting with someone negative, upset, or confused who is in your personal space."

This is a lifelong practice. And it has practical applications. You may be able to observe for yourself how others become calm and reasonable when you practice meditation.

In the beginning, I would also supplement IIH with the contemplation exercises in Bardon's third book on the cosmic language. I would not teach the cosmic letters the way Bardon does. Instead, for me, the cosmic letters embody what is already around and inside of us. They are the building blocks of matter, energy, life, consciousness, space, time, history, and spirit.

Consequently, you can create an energy field using the three senses concentration on a color, a sound, and an element. But you can also create the cosmic letter by working backwards. You can begin with contemplation on the themes of a specific cosmic letter. If you pursue this in-depth you create the same energy field you create by starting with a three sense concentration.

It would be like this: "For your next homework assignment this coming week, meditate on either the blue sky or the sea. For example, contemplate all the ways in which the sky is similar to an open and clear mind that embodies freedom. For example, notice how storms and weather appear within the sky and yet the sky is unaffected. Notice also the analogies between the flow of air in your chest and the winds and weather in the sky. Become the sky in your mind.

"Also contemplate the sea that brought life into being. Become the sea in your mind. Be aware of the fast variety of life forms that it nurtures and sustains. Sense also how water purifies, heals, absorbs and releases energy, and enables life to flourish."

In other words, right at the beginning, I would have students connect directly to nature. Earth, air, fire, and water are energies you master both in your body and in the biosphere. They are each infinitely rich in feeling, inspiration, and wisdom. (See my essay on Body awareness23).

Question 10

⊙

Due to your extensive work with elementals of the Water realm, for those who maybe have yet to experience their beauty can you please offer us an account of what it is like working with them.

B) What do you feel are the most important lessons you have learnt from them and how have you applied these lessons here?

William: In 2008, I put out a global casting call for women who could portray on a beach what a woman would be like if she embodied the energy of a mermaid. I did this because as I was editing my book, Undines, I noticed that two mermaid queens had promised me that I would meet mermaid spirits who inhabited human bodies. That is, you can have a human soul in a human body. You can also have in this case the soul of a mermaid in a woman's body. That is, she would have the one element of water composing her soul rather than the five elements that are typical of human souls.

Almost immediately after I started looking for such women I began running into them, getting referrals, and having them email me. Carefully

23 http://williammistele.com/body1.htm

interviewing these women, I summarized some of their qualities in my essay *Traits of Mermaid Women*[24] .

At least six times such women searched on the internet under "woman" and "mermaid" and found this essay and then emailed me. They often said, "It is like you are inside my head. You are the first person I have ever run into who understands who I am."

Previously, back in the 1990s, I had spent a fair amount of time meditating on and projecting into the astral realm of mermaids. There I met the four mermaid queens that Franz Bardon describes in his second book–Istiphul, Isaphil, Amue, and Osipeh. So I already had a strong sense of what the personalities and spiritual qualities of these beings are like. In other books I am working on, *Problems in the Study of Mermaids* and *Letters to Mermaids,* I discuss the problems that are inherent in these kinds of magical incarnations. When a mermaid incarnates in a human body, there is no manual next to her crib explaining what the human realm is like and what she can do here. Any being, no matter what its soul nature, still is under a prime directive governing all incarnations on earth. Namely, you get to choose for yourself what you wish to become. Even if a soul is only one element such as water, the human body has all five elements present in it. So such beings are free to involve themselves with life in any way they want.

However, the most common thing you notice with a mermaid personality with its pure water element is that they are incredibly empathic. They spontaneously feel what other people feel. If I ask one of them, "Tell me about so and so." They can instantly feel that individual's aura or astral body as if they are a part of that person. If you have a bell curve of seven billion people on earth, at one extreme are the psychopaths and dictators who exist only to maintain and acquire power. They are devoid of conscience or empathy.

At the other extreme of humanity are the incarnated mermaids. In their realm, there is no survival instinct. The vibration of the mermaid realm on the astral plane is pure love and pure innocence. They give all of themselves in every moment to everyone they meet. Being so innocent,

24 http://williammistele.com/finaltraits1019.htm

empathic, and giving, they usually have never met anyone like themselves.

So when they incarnate, they often are terribly abused. Even so, I have heard from some of them, "I have never had a mean thought in my life." And they often say, "I exist to love," and "I am one with the sea."

Now some human beings are also very empathic and clairsentient. The difference is that the incarnated mermaid, like the mermaid in her own realm, has no ego. If she relaxes and you put her next to the ocean, you can often notice that her aura blends with the sea. And so some of them say, "I am nature at the core of my being."

What follows from this is that possess astral immortality. In other words, if you study an element in nature so thoroughly that it becomes a part of yourself so that you feel you are one with nature, then you are joined from within to the biosphere of the planet earth. And that vast sea of energy is constantly renewing you so that your soul does not deteriorate and it also spontaneously regenerates itself.

Humans may have all five elements in their auras. But all five elements are defective. When humans reincarnate, their personalities are strongly influenced by their natal charts. When mermaids incarnate, they are the same person they were on the astral plane and in other lifetimes. They just learn new things from being here.

I am in contact with about thirty of these women. I have interviewed about twenty of them. And worked very closely with them almost on weekly basis, with about five of them. Due to the amount of contact, I have developed an immunity to the powerful attractive energies in their auras.

Typically, both men and women get "high" being near them. The strength of elemental water in their auras produces a cocaine effect. You feel larger than life around them. But when you move about fifty feet away, you may experience physical withdrawal symptoms like you feel half dead. But you are just returning to your normal energy level.

The water in a mermaid's aura is naturally rejuvenating. Its very nature is to make you feel fully alive. And so many of them are healers. They do not use the Bardon style dazzling bright light and condensed, the fiery form of vitality that Bardon initially presents in his books. Rather, they flow through you a soothing, relaxing, releasing, renewing, and invigorating kind of energy.

As I did with the mermaid queens on the astral plane, I often meditate with incarnated mermaids on the cosmic letter M from Bardon's third book on Kaballah. This is the "mother" letter and it embodies many of the magical qualities of the water element. Concentrating on this blue-green, cold, watery vibration is like creating the actual soul substance of mermaid queens. The queens' auras vibrate with and are connected to all water on earth and the magnetism of the biosphere. It is a very healing energy and working with it is also part of Bardon's training system.

For Bardon, the colder the sensation of water you can create the more magnetism you generate. I gave one of the mermaid women an electronic thermometer to test her ability to concentrate on cold. She held the thermometer in her hand and in the first try she was able to change the room temperature from 99 degrees Fahrenheit to 37 degrees Fahrenheit. Her son came into the room and told her the room was freezing. Some of these women are often born with many siddhis such as weather control.
On the other hand, our entire civilization is based on technology derived from fire and electricity. The mermaid personality has an enormous amount of empathy, and the ability to connect to any person on earth instantly and to feel what they feel inside–this kind of femininity is not present in human religions, wisdom traditions, theologies, or literature. In the past, such women have had to hide themselves in order not to be abused or killed.

So for me, one of Bardon's great contributions to human civilization is to point out that a student needs to master both the electric and magnetic fluids, (the masculine and feminine energies). But again, there is nothing in our culture that teaches us about this kind of femininity–the ability to be absolutely receptive and free of all ego and selfishness so that spontaneously and instantly you can feel a part of any living being on earth, as well as feeling joined from within to the water element in nature and on the astral plane.

If a woman wants to embody masculine energy (the electric fluid), she can certainly have a relationship with a man but she does not need a man.

All she needs to do in this present civilization is go get a job where she becomes a manager, a supervisor, or assume a command role. Then she does what men do–takes charge, oversees, produces and makes things, effects change, and masters all limitations of her environment or field of endeavor.

If a man wants to embody femininity in himself, to master the magnetic fluid which hermetic practice demands he does or he will be at a total loss. Do yoga, Taoist practices, martial arts, silence meditation, Vipassana, Dzogchen, Zen, Reiki, Tai Chi Chuan, etc.–none of these traditions has even a tiny clue about how to teach the magnetic fluid which is the very essence of the mermaid realm and the auras of mermaids.
But again, as I read Bardon, he is saying,

> *You are going to master the feminine mysteries of the water element and the magnetic fluid even if your world knows absolutely nothing about these things.*

In my mind, my four-year project to find a girl who could be on a beach and vibrate with the mermaid realm succeeded. My research is documented in *Mermaid Tales*.25

This young woman has the telekinetic ability to move small objects with her mind. She can control the weather to some extent. She can locate people by sensing where they are. And she can scan the entire human race nation by nation if I say to her, "Find me such and such a kind of person."

When I read a sentence about a spirit that Bardon describes, even before I am done reading, she sees the spirit walking through the wall and into the room. Like some of the other mermaid women, dead people appear to her as fully alive as living people. Her aura makes the dead feel as if they live again. I have some videos of her, Aaron, and myself describing the auras of the mermaid queens and the mermen Bardon describes in his second book, (View my video channel for more information).26

---

25 https://amzn.to/2Yv1ESg

26 https://www.youtube.com/user/Emedetz

All the same, as a disclaimer, I like to say, "Some women are too beautiful to love. It is best if you forget about them as if you have never met them. Or else, you must go on a journey, enter, and become a part of the realm from which they have come. Then their love becomes a part of your soul forever."

Franz Bardon warns his students several times to be careful with mermaid queens because the enchantment of love is so great in the magnetism of water they possess. To be honest, being around some of them requires that I be prepared at any moment to let go of the girl, as if I will never see her again. That kind of akashic detachment enables me to do my job as a spiritual anthropologist and really study what is in front of me. Otherwise, even the most rational of men are vulnerable to being overpowered by their own lower brain instinctual cravings around these women.

The greatest problem in studying the mermaid realm is that its pure innocence and it uninhibited and nearly divine empathic love is at complete odds with the world in which we live. We live in a world of scarcity–not enough food, housing, wealth, energy, and even affection and love are competed for and in scarce supply.

And not only that. The four elemental realms on earth do not communicate with each other. As I pointed out, if the salamander Orudu is going to set off a supervolcano, he does not hold a council with the mermaid queens, with the gnome kings, and with the sylphs. It is up to the trained magician to embody in his consciousness the kings and queens of the four elemental realms. As more individuals do so, the biosphere itself becomes more harmonious as does human society.

For example, when I have introduced incarnated mermaids to the salamander of lightning–Itumo–they fall in love with him. Being ultra-feminine, mermaids crave contact with masculine energy. And part of this Bardon explains. In IIH, Bardon presents the electro-magnetic volt. The magnetic fluid, again the feminine, surrounds the electric fluid–the masculine. This is the exact opposite of the world in which we live–the masculine culture for thousands of years has been oppressing and dominating women. In the electro-magnetic volt, the feminine–the magnetic fluid–surrounds, contains, refines, purifies, directs, and transforms the masculine energy. In effect, a magically trained woman can so unite with the soul of any man on earth that she can take all that he is and transform him into the man he is meant to be. Put simply, if you give anyone enough one on one attention, you have a good chance of getting them to do or become anything. That is the power of the feminine spirit.

For me, empathy and pure receptivity are the greatest power in this solar system. I explore that concept of the void as pure receptivity and empathy to dissolve negativity and establish justice on earth in my book, *The Perfection of Wisdom.*

Another way, I am applying what I have learned from mermaid women is through my meditations on the femininity in women's bodies. For me, men in all their relationships and experiences with women are still unable to internalize the femininity of women into themselves. But you can take each part of what makes a woman feminine, study the energy underlying her physical body and feminine vibration.

And then you can find in nature–in rain, clouds, rivers, streams, lakes, and oceans–images and vibrations that you can meditate on and use to create in yourself the receptivity, vivaciousness, bliss, nurturing qualities, soothing, releasing, rejuvenating, and empathy that ultra-feminine women possess. And then I add in the three sense concentrations of the cosmic language of Bardon's third book which are the basic building blocks of all energy in the universe.

This I have learned to do from working with mermaid women. When I create with my hand or mind a specific vibration, they can instantly feel what I feel. If I create and then say to a mermaid woman, "This is the vibration of your astral body and your physical body," they can give me immediate feedback on how accurate I am and how they experience it as compared to me.

By working with these energies in this way, everything she is becomes a part of me, and everything I am becomes a part of her. And that is the nature of magic–to observe with the clarity of a mirror and to become one with whatever you focus on.

QUESTION 11

⊙

IS THERE ANYTHING FURTHER YOU WOULD LIKE TO ADD?

William: I have some longer essays on my website27. (For example, *How to Speak to Saturn* and also *The Perfection of Wisdom)* for practices relating to dissolving negativity and also establishing justice between nations. Bardon places immense creative powers into our hands and his students will apply these skills in many ways.

Isaiah the prophet said,

> *They shall beat their swords into ploughshares, and their spears into pruning hooks: nation shall not lift up sword against nation, neither shall they learn war anymore.*

I am in love with that saying. But Isaiah left out the method.

I am supplying a viable method and continuously field testing it.

27 https://williamrmistele.com/

Made in the USA
Monee, IL
12 December 2022

b362ffdd-9ce3-4cb1-805b-12bef1304e37R01